A Daily Dose of Laughter

JIM KRAUS

Revell
a division of Baker Publishing Group

This edition published in 2013 by Hallmark Gift Books, a division of Hallmark Cards, Inc., Kansas City, MO 64141 under license from Baker Publishing Group.

Visit us on the Web at Hallmark.com.

Scripture quotations are from the Holy Bible, New International Version®. NIV®. Copyright © 1973, 1978, 1984, 2011 by Biblica, Inc.™ Used by permission of Zondervan. All rights reserved worldwide. www.zondervan.com

Illustrated by Maura Cluthe

ISBN: 978-1-59530-598-5
BOK1257

Printed and bound in China

To my wife and son, whose laughter is the most perfect medicine

PREFACE

I am writing this preface in hopes of preventing an avalanche of hate mail. Well, not hate mail, exactly. More like dislike mail. Or indignant mail. And this from a joke book of all things. What's the matter with us these days?

I've been collecting jokes for years, and I've pulled together some of my favorites. I hope you enjoy them. Within these pages are jokes that make fun of blondes, Catholics, Baptists, Vikings, Packers, old people, young people, army guys, Jewish people, Canadians, Norwegians, rabbis, preachers, popes, churchgoers, married people, golfers, cowboys, blondes . . . Wait, didn't I mention blondes before? I think I did. For the record, I used to be a blonde. Not that kind of blonde, though. And I am a churchgoer. And a married person.

So I am not offended by any of the blonde, married-person, churchgoer jokes. Please be assured that these are *jokes* and are not presumed to accurately portray said blonde or cowboy or blonde married person. Allow me to share an inconvenient truism with you—a lot of jokes just don't work if every stereotype is replaced with "some man" or "some woman."

So I am encouraging us all to hold our righteous indignation at bay . . . poke fun at each other . . . and laugh a little.

Thanks,
Jim Kraus

And visit my website, www.jimkraus.com. There is no particular reason to do so, but it would make me feel less lonely.

Susan was having a lot of problems trying to sell her old car because it had 250,000 miles on it.

One day she told her problem to a friend, who said, "There is a way to make the car easier to sell, but it's not legal."

"That doesn't matter," Susan whispered, "if only I can sell the car."

"Okay," Susan's friend said. "Here is the address of a friend of mine. He owns a car repair shop. Tell him I sent you, and he'll turn the counter in your car back to 50,000 miles. Then it should not be a problem to sell your car."

Susan quickly made the trip to the mechanic. Two weeks later, her friend asked Susan, "Did you sell your car?"

"No," Susan replied, "why should I? It only has 50,000 miles on it!"

BLOOPER

Pastor Grayson will lead a brown-bag seminar titled "How to Hold Effective One-Hour Meetings" from noon to 1:30 on Wednesday.

QUOTE

To his dog, every man is Napoleon. Hence the continued popularity of dogs.

My mother began getting calls from people who misdialed the similar number of a new computer repair business. Mom, who had had her number for years, asked the owner of the company to have the number changed. He refused.

The calls kept coming day and night. At first Mom tried to tell them they had called the wrong number—but more calls came. Then she started giving them advice, despite the fact that she knew nothing about computers.

Finally, Mom began telling the people who called that the company had gone out of business. Within a week, the computer repair company voluntarily changed its number.

BLOOPER

All went well on the adult camping trip last weekend—despite the low temperatures in the late 40s and early 50s.

QUOTE

One good thing about apathy is you don't have to exert yourself to show you're sincere about it.

· DAY ·

3

Every member of the Mensa organization has an IQ in the top 2 percent and has to pass a difficult test of logic and reasoning to be admitted. A few years ago, there was a Mensa convention in San Francisco, and several members ate dinner at a local café. While dining, they discovered that their salt shaker contained pepper and their pepper shaker contained salt. How could they swap the contents of the bottles without spilling them, using only the implements at hand? Clearly this was a job for these Mensa members.

The group debated and presented ideas and finally came up with a brilliant solution involving a napkin, a straw, and an empty saucer. They called the waitress over to dazzle her with their solution.

"Miss," they said, "we couldn't help but notice that the pepper shaker contains salt and the salt shaker—"

"Oh," the waitress interrupted. "Sorry about that." She unscrewed the caps of both bottles and switched them.

BLOOPER

Thanks! During our Summer Fest celebration, Mason's Funeral Home brought cheer to our senior citizens.

QUOTE

Appeasers believe that if you keep on throwing steaks to a tiger, the tiger will turn vegetarian.

· DAY ·

4

A woman and her husband had to interrupt their vacation to go to the dentist. "I want a tooth pulled, and I don't want any pain shots or Novocain because I'm in a big hurry," the woman said. "Just yank out the tooth as quickly as possible, and we'll be on our way."

The dentist was quite impressed. "You're certainly a courageous woman," he said. "Which tooth is it?"

The woman turned to her husband and said, "Show him your tooth, dear."

BLOOPER

The Granite City Men's Prayer Group will hold an early-riser breakfast. Breakfast will be served until 2:30 p.m.

QUOTE

A modern artist is one who throws paint on a canvas, wipes it off with a cloth, then sells the cloth.

At the banquet celebrating Tom and Susan's twenty-fifth wedding anniversary, Tom was asked to give his friends a brief account of the benefits of a long and successful marriage.

"Tell us, Tom," someone said, "just what is it you have learned from all those wonderful years with your wife?"

Tom responded, "Well, I've learned that marriage is the best teacher of all. It teaches you loyalty, forbearance, meekness, self-restraint, forgiveness—and a great many other qualities you wouldn't have needed if you'd stayed single."

BLOOPER

Company representative Chip Wallingsford spoke to the seniors at Gary Methodist Church and offered a free trial of the Miracle Ear hearing aid. "It's an unheard-of 60-day risk-free trial," he said.

QUOTE

An atheist is a man who has no invisible means of support.

While leading a tour of kindergarten students through the hospital, an X-ray technician was showing X-rays of broken bones.

"Have any of you ever broken a bone?" he asked.

A pretty little girl in pink raised her hand and replied, "I did."

"Did it hurt?" he asked.

"No," the little girl replied.

"Really? You must be a brave little girl. Which bone did you break?"

"My sister's arm."

BLOOPER

Associate Pastor Brian Husenut once again offered his guests smoked moose steak—"It's my own specialty of the horse."

QUOTE

A baby is God's opinion that the world should go on.

DAY 7

An eighty-five-year-old widow went on a blind date with a ninety-year-old man. When she returned to her daughter's house later that night, she seemed upset.

"What happened, Mother?" her daughter asked.

"I had to slap his face three times!"

"You mean he got fresh?" her daughter exclaimed, shocked and indignant.

"No," she answered, "I thought he was dead."

BLOOPER

The Swallow Falls Bible Church Monday night Bible study meets every Tuesday morning in the community room, except during July, when it meets on Wednesday night.

QUOTE

Show me a twin birth and I will show you an infant replay.

DAY 8

At the airport for a business trip, I settled down to wait for the boarding announcement at gate 35. Then I heard the voice on the public-address system say, "We apologize for the inconvenience, but Delta flight 570 will board from gate 41." So I picked up my luggage and hauled it over to gate 41.

Not ten minutes later the public-address voice told us that flight 570 would, in fact, be boarding from gate 35. So again I picked up my carry-on luggage and returned to the original gate.

Just as I was settling down, the public-address voice spoke again: "Thank you for participating in Delta's physical fitness program."

BLOOPER

Our Eden Valley Baptist Church softball team increased their record to 0-3.

QUOTE

Before you drink at a brook, it is well to know its source.

A man's car stalled on a country road. When he got out to fix it, a cow came along and stopped beside him. "Your trouble is probably in the carburetor," the cow said.

Startled, the man jumped back and ran down the road until he met a farmer. He told the farmer his story.

"Was it a large red cow with a brown spot over the right eye?" the farmer asked.

"Yes, yes," the man replied.

"Oh, I wouldn't listen to Bessie," the farmer said. "She doesn't know a thing about cars."

BLOOPER

The Edisons are renting out their "cute as a button" honeymoon cottage on Fishers Lake. Sleeps three.

QUOTE

Cheap things are not good; good things are not cheap.

My sister, a truck driver, decided to get a dog for protection. As she inspected a likely candidate, the trainer told her, "He doesn't like men at all." Perfect for protection, my sister thought, and bought the dog.

One day, two men in a parking lot approached her, and she watched to see how her canine bodyguard would react. Soon it became clear that the trainer wasn't kidding. As the men got closer, the dog ran under the nearest car.

BLOOPER

For sale: Electric hospital bed, hardly used. No one died in it.

QUOTE

Every boy who has a dog should also have a mother, so the dog can be fed regularly.

DAY 11

Pete and Gladys were looking at a new living room suite in the furniture store. Pete said to the salesman, "We really like it, but I don't think we can afford it."

"Don't worry," the salesman said. "You just make a small down payment, and then you don't make another payment for six months."

Gladys wheeled around with her hands on her hips and said, "Who told you about us?"

BLOOPER

Sarah Mickels posed the following question to the women's Bible study: "Do you want your child to go to college? Then must start with good education for sure."

QUOTE

Ask your child what he wants for dinner only if he's buying.

DAY 12

A crew of highway maintenance workers was sent to repair some road signs that vandals had knocked down in a forested area. The first one the workers put back up was a symbol warning of a deer crossing. As they moved down the road to repair the next sign, one crew member looked back and spotted a deer running across the highway. She turned to a co-worker and said, "I wonder how long he's been waiting to cross?"

BLOOPER

For sale: Wooden casket, turns into a picnic table, handmade.

QUOTE

One thing about children—they never go around showing off pictures of their grandparents.

This morning, my wife came into the kitchen and asked, "What are you doing today?"

"Nothing," I said.

Peeved, she said, "That's what you did yesterday."

I replied, "I wasn't finished."

BLOOPER

Speaking to the Pairs and Spares Seniors Group, Dr. Larson suggested that sunshine is good for prostate troubles.

QUOTE

I see where several of our politicians are predicting a return of prosperity as soon as business picks up.

In 1947 Milton Berle was one of the biggest names in comedy. But as his career rose, his marriage failed, leading to a divorce from his wife, Joyce Mathews. Two years later, Berle and Mathews got married for the second time. He was asked why he would marry the same woman all over again.

"Because," Berle said, "she reminds me of my first wife."

BLOOPER

Children's director Marshfield said, "Anything we assume now is just an assumption."

QUOTE

Early to bed, early to rise is a sure sign that you're fed up with television.

One day an employee came in to work with both of his ears bandaged. When his boss asked him what happened, he explained, "Yesterday I was ironing a shirt when the phone rang, and I accidentally answered the iron instead of the phone."

"Well," the boss said, "that explains one ear, but what about the other?"

"They called back!"

BLOOPER

Church latecomers are urged to sit on the main floor or upstairs in the baloney.

QUOTE

I did not attend his funeral. I sent a nice letter saying I approved of it.—*Mark Twain*

·DAY· 16

Two blondes hiked deep into the forest searching for a Christmas tree. After hours in the deep snow and biting wind, one blonde turned to the other and said, "I'm chopping down the next tree I see. I don't care whether it's decorated or not!"

BLOOPER

Summer Sunday school electives: Communication—how to make communicate more effective.

QUOTE

Everything has been said before, but since nobody listens we have to keep going back to the beginning all over again.

·DAY· 17

I felt like my body had gotten totally out of shape, so my doctor urged me to join a fitness club and start exercising. I decided to take an aerobics class for seniors. I bent, twisted, gyrated, jumped up and down, and perspired for an hour. But by the time I got my leotard on, the class was over.

BLOOPER

Dr. Shields reminded the parents of the youth group to remember the three Es: education, employment, accountability.

QUOTE

It's funny that a man hires someone to cut his grass so he can play golf for exercise.

·DAY· 18

I've sure gotten old. I've had two bypass surgeries, I've had a hip replacement, and I have new knees. I fought prostate cancer and diabetes. I'm half blind, can't hear anything quieter than a jet engine, and take forty different medications that make me dizzy, winded, and subject to blackouts. Have bouts with dementia. Have poor circulation—hardly feel my hands and feet anymore. Can't remember if I'm eighty-five or ninety-two. Have lost all my friends. But, thankfully, I still have my driver's license.

BLOOPER

Kevin Vetter led the youth group on a visit to St. Augustine, which was built 300 years ago by the Spaniels.

QUOTE

If pleasures are greatest in anticipation, just remember that this is also true of trouble.

Kentucky is not known as a state that has many hang-gliding enthusiasts. But Billy Bob Joe Hicks always wanted to try it and saved up enough money to buy a hang glider. He took it to the highest mountain near his home, and after struggling to the top, he got ready to take flight. He took off running, reached the edge of the cliff, jumped into the wind, and was airborne!

Meanwhile, Maw and Paw Hicks were on the porch swing talking about the good old days when Maw spotted the biggest bird she had ever seen. "Look at the size of that bird, Paw!" she exclaimed.

Paw straightened up and said, "Fetch my gun, Maw."

She ran into the house and brought out his shotgun. He took careful aim. *Bang! Bang! Bang! Bang!*

The monster-sized bird continued to sail silently over the treetops.

"I think you missed him, Paw," Maw said.

"I did," he replied, "but at least he let go of Billy Bob Joe!"

BLOOPER

The Kids on Wheels skateboard demonstration was graciously sponsored by the Brain Injury Counsel of West Branch.

QUOTE

It would have helped if the pioneers had located cities closer to airports.

My first stop on my vacation was my sister's house in Montana. She's extremely organized—to the utmost degree. Before she leaves on a trip, she always types up address labels for her postcards.

This time, I figured I'd done her one better. I boasted, "You'll be impressed. I've already written thank-you notes to everyone with whom I'll be staying. They're all stamped and ready to go."

My sister was silent for a moment, and then she said, "You mean those little envelopes I saw in your room and mailed this morning?"

BLOOPER

The youth group will be selling real Italian sub sandwiches made with important provolone cheese.

QUOTE

The only thing worse than hearing the alarm clock in the morning is not hearing it.

·DAY· 21

Al and Lois go to a counselor after fifteen years of marriage. The counselor asks them what the problem is. Lois goes into a tirade, listing every problem they've ever had in their years of marriage. She goes on and on and on.

Finally, the counselor gets up, embraces the surprised Lois, and kisses her passionately.

Lois shuts up and sits quietly in a daze.

The counselor turns to Al and says, "That is what your wife needs at least three times a week. Can you do that?"

Al thinks for a moment and replies, "Well, I can get her here Mondays and Wednesdays, but Fridays I play golf."

BLOOPER

Order Dr. Rost's complete series, "End Times and Its Aftermath." You need this now! (Allow 8 to 12 weeks for delivery.)

QUOTE

Age is a high price to pay for maturity.

·DAY· 22

Five-year-old Logan and his family were having Thanksgiving dinner at his grandmother's house. Everyone was seated around the table as the food was being served. When little Logan received his plate, he started eating right away.

"Logan, wait until we say our prayer," his mother reminded him.

"I don't need to," the little boy replied.

"Of course you do!" his mother insisted. "We say a prayer before eating at our house."

"That's at our house," Logan explained, "but this is Grandma's house, and she knows how to cook!"

BLOOPER

The Church Madrigals and Theater Group will present "An Evening in the Little House on the Prairie." Experience life as it was in the 1970s.

QUOTE

The one good thing about egotists is that they don't go around talking about other people.

While Miss Williams's third-grade class was completing a writing exercise, one of the students asked the teacher how to spell *piranha*.

She told him she wasn't sure. To her delight, he headed straight to the dictionary.

That's when she overheard another student say to him, "Why bother to look it up? She doesn't know how to spell it anyway."

BLOOPER

Performing tonight at the Sunday evening Singspiration are the Chase twins. Holly is 9 and Heather is 7.

QUOTE

The cards are badly shuffled until I get a good hand.

Hazel, a recent widow, requested the epitaph "Rest in Peace" for her husband's tombstone. When Hazel later found out he had left his fortune to his mistress, she attempted to get the engraver to change the carving. This was impossible; the words were chiseled and could not be changed.

"In that case," Hazel said, "please add 'Till We Meet Again.'"

BLOOPER

Cleo Haster reminds the men in the church to prepare for Mother's Day. This year, for all church men, she is offering a Mother's Day special: free tick and flea bath.

QUOTE

A bore is a man who deprives you of solitude without providing you with company.

·DAY· 25

The orthopedic surgeon Betty worked for was moving to a new office, and the staff was helping transport many of the items.

Betty sat the display skeleton in the front of her car, his bony arm across the back of her seat. She hadn't considered the drive across town. At one traffic light, the stares of the people in the car beside her became obvious, and she looked across and explained, "I'm delivering him to my doctor's office."

The driver leaned out his window. "I hate to tell you, lady," he said, "but I think it's too late!"

BLOOPER

It's summer in Johnstown, and the Johnstown Hills Baptist Church and the Poison Control Center of Summit County remind kids not to take poison this summer.

QUOTE

Business is like a bicycle—either you keep moving or you fall down.

·DAY· 26

Stan, a contestant on a TV game show, was only 100 points behind the leader and was set to answer the final question—worth 250 points!

"To be today's champion," the show's host said, "name two of Santa's reindeer."

Stan gave a sigh of relief, gratified that he had drawn such an easy question. "Rudolph!" he said confidently. "And . . . Olive!"

The studio audience started to applaud, but the clapping was quickly replaced by mumbling and embarrassed giggles. The confused host replied, "Yes, we'll accept Rudolph, of course, but there is no reindeer named Olive."

"There is too," Stan argued. Instead of explaining his answer, he began to sing, "Rudolph the Red-Nosed Reindeer had a very shiny nose. And if you ever saw it, you would even say it glows. *Olive*, the other reindeer . . ."

BLOOPER

Nearly half of the Community Gospel Church cannot say if the elder board is indecisive.

QUOTE

The real trouble with reality is that there is no background music.

A teenager is . . .

Someone who can't remember to walk the dog each day but never forgets a phone number he heard once.

A weight watcher who goes on a diet by giving up candy bars before breakfast.

Someone who receives her allowance on Monday, spends it on Tuesday, and borrows it from her best friend on Wednesday.

Someone who can pick out the voice of a friend from three blocks away but can't hear his mother calling from the next room.

A computer whiz who can operate any new gadget within seconds but can't make the bed.

A connoisseur of two types of fine music: loud and very loud.

A romantic who never falls in love more than twice a week.

His own reality show but with fewer commercials.

Painfully funny at many times. At other times, just painful.

Someone who will pitch in and help clean every room in the house, as long as it's the neighbor's house.

BLOOPER

Susan Howell, children's ministry director, has the following tip for new parents: "Show your children that you care. Start off by learning each of their names."

QUOTE

Going to church does not make you a Christian any more than standing in a garage makes you a car.

· DAY ·

28

Lewis, an eight-year-old boy, was an eyewitness to a crime and was called to testify in court. He was approached by the defense attorney, who asked, "Did anyone tell you what to say in court?"

"Yes, sir," Lewis answered.

"I thought so," the attorney said. "Who was it?"

"My father, sir."

"And what did he tell you?" the attorney asked accusingly, thinking that he had trapped the young boy, therefore disqualifying his testimony.

"He said that the lawyers would try to get me all tangled up, but if I told the truth, everything would be all right."

BLOOPER

A visiting health nurse told the Bible study group to take extra precautions with elderly in heat.

QUOTE

Everyone is entitled to be foolish sometimes, but many people abuse the privilege.

· DAY ·

29

A new hair salon opened for business right across the street from Leo's, the town's long-established barbershop.

The owners of the new salon put up a big, bold sign that read: "WE GIVE SEVEN-DOLLAR HAIRCUTS!"

Not to be outdone, Leo, the barber with forty years of experience, put up his own sign: "WE FIX SEVEN-DOLLAR HAIRCUTS!"

BLOOPER

Church bulletin board: If birds could build their own nests, they would look like Mrs. Adam's woven creations.

QUOTE

If pro is the opposite of con, then what is the opposite of progress?

Two women came before wise king Solomon, dragging between them a young man in a three-piece suit.

"This young lawyer agreed to marry my daughter," one said.

"No! He agreed to marry *my* daughter," the other said.

They haggled before the king until he called for silence.

"Bring me my biggest sword," Solomon said, "and I shall hew the young attorney in half. Each of you shall receive a half."

"Sounds good to me," the first lady said.

But the second woman said, "Oh, sire, do not spill innocent blood. Let the other woman's daughter marry him."

The wise king did not hesitate a moment. "The attorney must marry the first lady's daughter," he proclaimed.

"But she was willing to hew him in two!" the king's court exclaimed.

"Indeed," wise king Solomon said. "That shows she is the *true* mother-in-law."

BLOOPER

Church Swap Corner: Would like to trade a 9 x 13 pan for a 13 x 9 pan.

QUOTE

A train station is where a train stops. A bus station is where a bus stops. On my desk, I have a work station.

DAY 31

A high-ranking Mafia "businessman" finds out that Paul, his bookkeeper, has cheated him out of $10 million.

Paul has been deaf all his life. That was the reason he got the job in the first place. It was assumed that a deaf bookkeeper would not hear anything that he might have to testify about in court.

When the Mafia businessman goes to confront the bookkeeper about his missing $10 million, he brings along his attorney, who knows sign language.

The mobster tells the lawyer, "Ask him where the $10 million he embezzled from me is."

The attorney, using sign language, asks the bookkeeper where the money is.

The bookkeeper signs back, "I don't know what you are talking about."

"He says he doesn't know what you're talking about," the attorney tells the godfather.

The godfather pulls out a pistol, puts it to the bookkeeper's temple, and says, "Ask him again!"

The attorney signs to the bookkeeper, "He'll kill you if you don't tell him!"

Paul signs back, "Okay, you win! The money is in a brown briefcase, buried behind the shed in my cousin Enzo's backyard in Queens!"

"Well, what'd he say?" the godfather asks the attorney.

The attorney replies, "He says you don't have the guts to pull the trigger."

BLOOPER

Forty percent of the children in our under-12 Sunday school class are under 12—up from 30 percent last year.

QUOTE

If you think things cannot get worse, it is probably because you lack sufficient imagination.

DAY 32

You might be a preacher if . . .

You've been asked, as often as weekly, "What's so hard about preaching?"

Others wished they worked only one day a week for a week's pay!

You have ever said, "I'm *never* going to be a preacher!"

You wear your new shoes to church and someone comments, "We are paying you too much money!"

Women call up and say they want you to marry them.

You keep relating movies you've seen to sermon topics.

You name your bed "the Word." (You tell everyone that you "stay in the Word.")

You jiggle all the commode handles at the church before you leave.

Instead of being "ticked off," you get "grieved in your spirit."

You've ever dreamed you were preaching only to awaken and discover you were.

BLOOPER

Church bulletin board: Chi wau wau puppies for sale.

QUOTE

Knowledge is realizing that the street is a one-way street, and wisdom is looking in both directions anyway.

· DAY ·
33

Old aunts used to come up to me at weddings, poke me in the ribs, and cackle, telling me, "You're next."

They stopped after I started doing the same thing to them at funerals.

BLOOPER

Elder Duncan said that there are 24 trees on the church property that need to be completely cut and removed, owing to their current condition of not being alive.

QUOTE

Expecting the world to treat you fairly because you are a good person is like expecting the bull not to charge you because you are a vegetarian.

DAY 34

Murphy and his wife, Ann, a middle-aged couple, went for a stroll in the park. They sat down on a bench to rest.

Then they overheard voices coming from a secluded spot.

Suddenly Mrs. Murphy realized that a young man was about to propose. Not wanting to eavesdrop on such an intimate moment, she nudged her husband and whispered, "Whistle and let that young couple know that someone can hear them."

"Whistle?" Murphy said. "Why should I whistle? Nobody whistled to warn me!"

BLOOPER

Church constitution update: A congregationally approved measure for congregational approval does not require a congregational vote by the congregation.

QUOTE

You can't be late until you show up.

DAY 35

Charlie had an hour before his flight to Los Angeles. He decided to kill some time at an airport coffee shop. He walked in and sat down next to a clearly nervous guy, who had three empty latte cups in front of him. Charlie introduced himself to the guy and bought him a cup of tea.

"Nervous about flying?" Charlie asked.

The guy replied, "N-nervous? I'm t-terrified. I just know the p-plane is going t-to crash and we're g-going to d-die."

"Is this your first time flying?"

"N-no, I fly c-cross-country all the t-time. It's m-my job."

"Why don't you just ask your boss if you can drive cross-country?"

"H-he would never l-let me do that."

"Why not?" Charlie asked.

The nervous guy replied, "B-because I'm the p-pilot."

The Bikers for Christ will head to Milwaukee for the Hardley Davidson tour next week.

The secret to creativity is knowing how to hide your sources.

· DAY ·
36

One afternoon Herb was walking on a trail with his infant daughter, chatting to her about the scenery.

When a man and his dog approached, Herb leaned down to the carriage and said, "See the doggy?" Suddenly he felt foolish talking to his baby as if she understood him.

However, just as the man passed, he reached down, patted his dog, and said, "See the baby?"

Church bulletin board—For rent: Swansea Apartments—half off the first month's rent. No poets, please.

It isn't homework unless it's due tomorrow.

· DAY · 37

Fatal things to say if your wife's pregnant:

I finished the last of the Oreos.

Not to imply anything, but I don't think the kid weighs forty pounds.

You know, looking at her, you'd never guess that Pamela Lee had a baby.

I sure hope your thighs aren't going to stay that flabby forever.

Well, couldn't they induce labor? You do realize that you're due on Super Bowl Sunday . . .

Fred at the office passed a stone the size of a pea. Boy, that had to hurt.

I'm jealous. Why can't men experience the joy of childbirth?

Are your ankles supposed to look like that?

Get your *own* ice cream.

Gee, you're awfully puffy-looking today.

Maybe we should name the baby after my secretary. Tawney is a nice name.

Man! That rose tattoo on your hip is the size of Madagascar!

Retaining water? Yeah, like the Hoover Dam retains water.

Your stomach sticks out almost as much as your rear!

You don't have the guts to pull that trigger.

BLOOPER

Church bulletin board: Symease kittens for sale or adoptions.

QUOTE

Parents spend the first part of their children's lives teaching them to walk and talk, and then the rest of it telling them to sit down and be quiet.

· DAY · 38

My husband works as a service technician for a large exterminating company. One of the rules of the company is that he has to confirm each appointment by phone the night before his service call to that household.

One evening he made such a call, and when a man answered the phone, he said, "Hi, this is Gary from A to Z Pest Control Company. Your wife phoned us."

There was a long silence, and then Gary heard the man on the other end say, "Honey, it's for you. Someone wants to talk to you about your relatives."

Church bulletin board: Tricycle for sale—with training wheels.

Books have knowledge, knowledge is power, power corrupts, corruption is a crime, crime doesn't pay—so if you keep reading, you'll go broke.

· DAY ·
39

A somewhat advanced society has figured out how to package all basic knowledge in pill form. A student, needing some learning, goes to the pharmacy and asks what kind of knowledge pills are available.

The pharmacist says, "Here's a pill for English literature." The student takes the pill, swallows it, and has new knowledge about English literature.

"What else do you have?" the student asks.

"Well, I have pills for art history, biology, and world history," the pharmacist replies.

The student asks for these, swallows them, and has new knowledge about those subjects. Then the student asks, "Do you have a pill for math?"

The pharmacist says, "Wait just a moment," and goes back into the storeroom. He brings back a whopper of a pill the size of a hamburger bun and plunks it on the counter.

"I have to take that huge pill for math?" the student asks.

The pharmacist replies, "Well, you know . . . math always was a little hard to swallow."

Health expert Jan Peale told our women's group that studies have found that fatigue sets in late in the day.

As long as there are pop quizzes in school, there will be prayer in school.

·DAY·
40

Suzanne, a cheerful blonde woman, enters a store that sells curtains. She tells the salesman, "I would like to buy a pair of pink curtains."

The salesman assures Suzanne that they have a large selection of pink curtains. He shows her several patterns, but the blonde seems to have a hard time choosing. Finally, she selects a lovely pink floral print. The salesman then asks what size curtains she needs.

"Fifteen inches," Suzanne replies.

"Fifteen inches?" the salesman asks. "That sounds very small. What room are they for?"

Suzanne tells him that they aren't for a room but are for her computer monitor.

The surprised salesman says, "But, miss, computers don't need curtains!"

Suzanne replies, drawing out the words, "Hellooo! I've got Windows!"

BLOOPER

Big, Beautiful Woman member Pat Tyson returned from Washington and said that pro-fat groups are bigger and more visible.

QUOTE

You know your god is man-made when he hates all the same people you do.

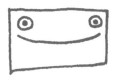

One day a little girl came home from school and said to her mother, "Mommy, today in school I was punished for something I didn't do."

The mother exclaimed, "That's terrible! I'm going to have a talk with your teacher about this. By the way, what was it you didn't do?"

The little girl replied, "My homework."

BLOOPER

Pastor Hurley spoke to the father/son group before their annual camping trip and told them that in order to survive a lightning strike, it is best if you avoid getting hit by lightning.

QUOTE

Advice for the day: if you have a headache, do what it says on the aspirin bottle. "Take two, and keep away from children."

George Phillips was going up to bed when his wife told him that he'd left the light on in the garden shed, which she could see from the bedroom window. George opened the back door to turn off the light but saw that there were people in the shed, stealing his things.

He phoned the police, who asked, "Is an intruder in your house?" and he said no. They said that all patrols were busy, and that he should simply lock his door and an officer would be along when available. George hung up, counted to thirty, and phoned the police again.

"Hello, I just called you a few seconds ago because there were people in my shed. Well, you don't have to worry about them now because I've just shot them." Then he hung up.

Within a minute, three police cars, an Armed Response Unit, and an ambulance showed up at the Phillips residence. Of course, the police caught the burglars red-handed.

"I thought you said that you shot them!" one of the policemen said to George.

George replied, "I thought you said there was nobody available!"

BLOOPER

Dr. Wilcox will help explore your pashion for writing in his sedminar on Good Christian Writing.

QUOTE

Love is like the number pi—natural, irrational, and very important.

An Irishman in a wheelchair entered a restaurant one afternoon and asked the waitress for a cup of coffee. He looked across the restaurant and asked, "Is that Jesus sitting over there?" The waitress nodded, so the Irishman told her to give Jesus a cup of coffee on him.

The next patron to come in was an Englishman with a hunched back. He shuffled over to a booth, sat down, and asked the waitress for a cup of hot tea. He also glanced across the restaurant and asked, "Is that Jesus over there?" The waitress nodded, so the Englishman said to give Jesus a cup of hot tea. "My treat."

The third patron to come into the restaurant was a redneck on crutches. He hobbled over to a booth, sat down, and hollered, "Hey there, sweet thang! How's about getting me a cold glass of Coke?" He too looked across the restaurant and asked, "Is that God's boy over there?" The waitress nodded once more, so the redneck said to give Jesus a cold glass of Coke. "And put it on my bill."

As Jesus got up to leave, he passed by the Irishman, touched him, and said, "For your kindness, you are healed." The Irishman felt the strength come back into his legs, got up, and danced a jig out the door.

Jesus also passed by the Englishman, touched him, and said, "For your kindness, you are healed." The Englishman felt his back straightening up, and he raised his hands, praised the Lord, and did a series of backflips out the door.

Then Jesus walked toward the redneck. The redneck jumped up and yelled, "Don't touch me! I'm drawing disability!"

BLOOPER

Our elder board reported that they have been encouraged to note that the city of Ames Corners has begun targeting fake fortune-tellers.

QUOTE

Optimism is waiting for a ship to come in when you haven't sent one out.

While I was working as a pediatric nurse, I had the difficult assignment of giving immunization shots to children. One day I entered the examining room to give four-year-old Lizzie her shot.

"No! No! No!" she screamed.

"Lizzie," her mother scolded, "that's not polite behavior."

At that, the girl yelled even louder, "No thank you! No thank you! No thank you!"

BLOOPER

Church bulletin board: Cordova Summer Bible Camp—lifeguards needed. Ability to swim a plus.

QUOTE

The shortest distance between two points is under construction.

A driver is stopped in heavy traffic in New York and says, "Wow, this traffic seems worse than usual. We're not even moving." Noticing a police officer walking down the highway between the cars, the man rolls down his window and says, "Excuse me, officer. Do you know what the holdup is?"

"It's our state senator—the one just convicted of taking bribes."

"Why would that stop traffic?" the driver asked.

"Well, he's all depressed by the news reports calling him a cheat and a liar," the cop replied. "He's lying down in the middle of the highway and threatening to douse himself in gasoline and light himself on fire because now he's flat broke and out of a job. I'm walking around taking up a collection for him."

"A collection, huh? How much have you got so far?" the man says.

"So far . . . ten gallons."

BLOOPER

Pairs and Spares topic of the month: Seniors—a secret source of meat.

QUOTE

It may look like I'm doing nothing, but I am actively waiting for my problems to go away.

DAY 46

One day a twelve-year-old boy was walking down the street when a car pulled up beside him and the driver lowered the window. "I'll give you a large bag of M&M's if you get in the car," the driver said.

"No way! Get lost!" the boy replied.

"How about a bag of candy and ten dollars?" the driver asked.

"I said no way."

"What about a bag of M&M's and fifty dollars?"

"No, I'm not getting in the car," the boy said.

"Okay, I'll give you a bag of M&M's and a hundred dollars," the driver offered.

"No!" the boy replied.

"What will it take to get you in the car?" the driver asked.

The boy replied, "Listen, Dad, you bought the purple minivan—you live with it!"

BLOOPER

Swenden's annual festival opens with Mayor Higgins and the ceremonial cutting of the cheese.

QUOTE

Anyone who uses the phrase "as easy as taking candy from a baby" has never tried to take candy from a baby.

DAY 47

A pipe burst in a doctor's house, and he called a plumber. The plumber arrived, unpacked his tools, did mysterious plumber-type things for a while, and handed the doctor a bill for $600.

"This is ridiculous!" the doctor exclaimed. "Even I don't make that much as a doctor!"

The plumber waited for him to finish sputtering and fuming, then quietly said, "Neither did I when I was a doctor."

BLOOPER

Church bulletin board—For sale: Shandelier—10 arms in great condition.

QUOTE

Never interrupt your opponent when he's making a mistake.

During a wedding rehearsal, the groom approached the pastor with an unusual offer.

"Look, I'll give you a hundred dollars if you'll change the wedding vows. For the part where I'm to promise to 'love, honor, and obey' and 'be faithful to her forever, forsaking all others,' I'd appreciate it if you'd just leave that part out." He passed the minister a hundred-dollar bill and walked away satisfied.

The next day during the wedding ceremony, the time came for the bride and groom to exchange their vows. The pastor looked the young man in the eye and said, "Will you promise to prostrate yourself before her, obey her every command and wish, serve her breakfast in bed every morning of your life, and swear eternally before God and your lovely wife that you will not ever even look at another woman, as long as you both shall live?"

The groom gulped, looked around, and said in a tiny voice, "Yes." He then leaned toward the pastor and hissed, "I thought we had a deal."

The pastor put the hundred-dollar bill back into the groom's hand and whispered, "She made me a much better offer."

BLOOPER

At the monthly men's gathering, Derrick Larson will tell his story of being robbed at gumpoint.

QUOTE

War does not determine who is right. War determines who is left.

Top ten things only women understand:

10. Why it's good to have five pairs of black shoes.
9. The difference between cream, ivory, and off-white.
8. That crying can be fun.
7. Fat clothes.
6. How a salad, a diet drink, and a hot fudge sundae make a balanced lunch.
5. Why discovering a designer dress on the sale rack can be considered a peak life experience.
4. The inaccuracy of every bathroom scale ever made.
3. That a good man might be hard to find, but a good hairdresser is next to impossible.
2. Why a phone call between two women never lasts under ten minutes.
1. Other women!

BLOOPER

Dr. Norris reported that a study shows that castration cures male pattern baldness.

QUOTE

You can go anywhere you want in a lab coat, looking serious, and carrying a clipboard.

Church football explained:

Quarterback Sneak—Church members quietly leaving during the invitation.

Draw Play—What many children do with the bulletin during worship.

Halftime—The period between Sunday school and worship when many choose to leave.

Benchwarmer—Those who do not sing, pray, work, or do anything but sit.

Backfield in Motion—Making a trip to the back (restroom or water fountain) during the service.

Staying in the Pocket—What happens to a lot of money that should be given to the Lord's work.

Two-Minute Warning—The point at which you realize the sermon is almost over and begin to gather up your children and belongings.

Instant Replay—The preacher loses his notes and falls back on last week's illustrations.

Sudden Death—What happens to the attention span of the congregation if the preacher goes into overtime.

Trap—You're called on to pray and are nearly asleep.

End Run—Getting out of church quickly, without speaking to any guest or fellow member.

Flex Defense—The ability to allow absolutely nothing said during the sermon to affect your life.

Halfback Option—The decision of 50 percent of the congregation not to return for the evening service.

Blitz—The rush for the restaurants following the closing prayer.

BLOOPER

Seven of the nine elders voted unanimously to purchase a new church bus.

QUOTE

You can never learn anything by doing it right.

·DAY·
51

"Please, Your Honor, I'd like to be excused from jury duty today," pleaded Leroy, an anxious-looking man.

"Why should I excuse you?" the judge asked.

"You see, I owe a man one hundred dollars, and he's leaving in a few hours for a missionary job overseas," Leroy explained. "He'll be in the deep jungle for years, and I want to catch him before he leaves, for it may be my last chance to repay him."

"Excused," the judge stated coldly. "We don't want anyone on the jury who can lie like that."

BLOOPER

Self-Help Group Network asks local churches for help.

QUOTE

The speaker, drawing on his fine command of the English language, said nothing.

·DAY·
52

Two friends met in the street. Burt looked rather forlorn and down in the mouth. His friend Ted asked, "Hey, how come you look like the whole world caved in?"

"Let me tell you," Burt said. "Three weeks ago, an uncle died and left me $10,000."

"I'm sorry to hear about his death, but a bit of good luck for you, eh?"

"Hold on, I'm just getting started. Two weeks ago, a cousin I never knew kicked the bucket and left me $20,000, free and clear."

"Well, you can't be disappointed with that!" Ted said.

"Yep. But last week my grandfather passed away," Burt went on. "I inherited almost $100,000."

"Incredible! So how come you look so glum?"

"Well, this week . . . nothing!"

BLOOPER

Church bulletin board: The church is looking for self-starting, goat-oriented, talented people.

QUOTE

A criminal is a person with predatory instincts who does not have sufficient capital to form a corporation.

·DAY·
53

A guy sees a buddy and notices that his car is a total wreck. It's covered with leaves, grass, branches, dirt, and blood.

He asks his friend, "What happened to your car?"

"Well," his friend responds, "I ran into the lawyer who did my wife's divorce."

"Okay," the man says, "that explains the blood, but what about the leaves, the grass, the branches, and the dirt?"

"Well, I had to chase him all through the park."

BLOOPER

Dr. Bennett is offering a free ice scraper with every colonoscopy to church members.

QUOTE

Every rule has an exception. Especially this one.

A large, well-established Canadian lumber camp advertised that they were looking for a good lumberjack.

The very next day, a skinny little man showed up at the camp with his ax and knocked on the head lumberjack's door. The lumberjack took one look at the little man and told him to leave.

"Just give me a chance to show you what I can do," the skinny man said.

"Okay, see that giant redwood over there?" the lumberjack said. "Take your ax and go cut it down."

The skinny man headed for the tree, and in five minutes he was back, knocking on the lumberjack's door. "I cut the tree down," he said.

The lumberjack couldn't believe his eyes. "Where did you get the skill to chop down trees like that?"

"In the Sahara Forest," the man replied.

"You mean the Sahara Desert," the lumberjack said.

The man laughed and answered back, "Oh, sure, that's what they call it now!"

BLOOPER

The youth group will be selling pizza for two days only—Thursday, Friday, Saturday, Sunday.

QUOTE

Confession may be good for the soul, but it's not so good on your reputation.

55

The following is a series of ads that appeared in the *Times-Gazette*, a small-town newspaper:

> MONDAY: For sale: R. D. Jones has one sewing machine for sale. Phone 948-0707 after 7 p.m. and ask for Mrs. Kelly who lives with him cheap.
>
> TUESDAY: There was a mistake in my ad yesterday. It should have read, "One sewing machine for sale cheap. Phone 948-0707 and ask for Mrs. Kelly, who lives with him after 7 p.m."
>
> WEDNESDAY: I have received several annoying telephone calls because of the error made in the classified ad yesterday. The ad stands correct as follows: "For sale: R. D. Jones has one sewing machine for sale. Cheap. Phone 948-0707 after 7 p.m. and ask for Mrs. Kelly who loves with him."
>
> THURSDAY: I, R. D. Jones, have no sewing machine for sale. I smashed it. Don't call 948-0707, as I have had the phone disconnected. I have not been carrying on with Mrs. Kelly. Until yesterday she was my housekeeper, but she quit!

BLOOPER

Trinity Brethren Church: We care . . . because we care.

QUOTE

If the grass is greener in your neighbor's yard, you can bet his water bill is higher.

56

A good friend of mine warned me that, as my three daughters became old enough to date, I'd disapprove of every young man who took them out.

But when the time came, I was pleased that my friend's prediction was wrong. Each boy was pleasant and well mannered.

Talking to my daughter Joanna one day, I said that I liked all the young men she and her sisters brought home.

"You know, Dad," she replied, "we don't show you everybody."

BLOOPER

Church bulletin board: Bad mitten set for sale.

QUOTE

An American is a person who isn't afraid to call the president a jerk—but is always polite to the policeman who stops his car.

Mark, a newlywed, wants to get Sharon, his beautiful blonde wife, something nice for their first wedding anniversary, so he decides to buy her a cell phone. Sharon is excited—she loves her phone. Mark shows it to her and carefully and clearly explains all the features on the phone.

The next day Sharon goes shopping. Her phone rings and it's Mark.

"Hi, honey," Mark says. "How do you like your new phone?"

"I just love it," Sharon replies. "It's so small and your voice is as clear as a bell. But there's one thing I don't understand."

"What's that, baby?" Mark asks.

"How did you know I was at Walmart?"

BLOOPER

Samantha Reynolds, who spoke on the condition of her identity remaining secret, said being a Mormon was difficult.

QUOTE

If you look like your passport picture, you probably need the trip.

DAY 58

All I need to know about life I learned from a cow:

Wake up in a happy moood.

Don't cry over spilled milk.

Turn the udder cheek and mooove on.

Seize every opportunity and milk it for all it's worth!

It's better to be seen and not herd.

Honor thy fodder and thy mother and all your udder relatives.

Never take any bull from anybody.

Always let them know who's the bossy.

Black and white is always an appropriate fashion statement.

Don't forget to cownt your blessings every day.

BLOOPER

On their tour of the Mideast, Pastor Phillips and his wife saw many places that no longer exist.

QUOTE

If a man wants to keep a true perspective on his importance, he should have a dog that will worship him and a cat that will ignore him.

DAY 59

Charlie was a regular visitor at the racetrack. One afternoon he noticed an unusual sight. Right before the first race, a Catholic priest visited one of the horses in the stable area and gave it a blessing. Charlie watched the horse race very carefully, and the blessed horse came in first!

Charlie followed the priest before the next race, and again he went to the stables and performed a similar procedure. Charlie played a hunch and put a couple of dollars on the blessed horse. Sure enough, the blessed horse came in by two lengths, and Charlie won close to fifty bucks.

The priest continued the same procedure through the next few races, and Charlie won each time. He was now ahead $1,000, so between races Charlie left the track, went to the bank, and withdrew his life's savings—$20,000.

The biggest race of the day was the last one. Charlie followed the priest and watched carefully which horse he blessed. He then went to the betting window and put his whole $21,000 bundle of cash on that horse.

Then Charlie went out to watch the race. Down the stretch they came, and as they crossed the finish line, the horse Charlie bet on was dead last!

Charlie was crushed. He located the priest and told him that he had been watching him bless the horses all day, and they all were winners except the last horse, on which he had bet his life savings. Charlie asked, "What happened to the last horse you blessed? Why didn't it win like the others?"

"That's the trouble with you Protestants," the priest said. "You can never tell the difference between a blessing and the last rites."

BLOOPER

All absentee ballots for the office of church elder must be presented in person to the church elders.

QUOTE

Love is staying up all night with a sick child, or a healthy adult.

Two elderly Jewish men were sitting in a wonderful deli, with a mostly Jewish clientele, in New York City. The old men spoke Yiddish, the language of Jews who emigrated from Eastern Europe.

A Chinese waiter, who had been in New York for less than a year, came up to them, and in fluent, impeccable Yiddish, he asked them if everything was okay and if they were enjoying the holiday.

The Jewish men were dumbfounded. *Where did he ever learn such perfect Yiddish?* they both thought. After they paid the bill, they asked the restaurant manager, "Where did our waiter learn such fabulous Yiddish?"

The manager looked around, leaned in so no one else could hear, and said, "Shh, he thinks we're teaching him English."

BLOOPER

Edna Mae Taylor, now 22 months pregnant, will be leaving her responsibilities as choir director at the end of the month. Best wishes on your new endeavor, Edna.

QUOTE

The old believe everything, the middle-aged suspect everything, the young know everything.

61 An elderly woman decided to prepare her will and told her preacher she had two final requests. First, she wanted to be cremated, and second, she wanted her ashes scattered over Walmart.

"Walmart?" the preacher exclaimed. "Why Walmart?"

"Then I'll be sure my daughters will visit me twice a week."

BLOOPER

The ecumenical sunrise service at North Park was a great success. More than a dozen different abominations gathered together to worship.

QUOTE

To appreciate heaven, it's good for a person to experience fifteen minutes of hell.

62 You might be having a redneck Thanksgiving if:

Thanksgiving dinner is on a ping-pong table.

Thanksgiving dinner is squirrel and dumplings.

You're reusing your paper plates.

You have a complete set of salad bowls that all say Cool Whip on the side.

You're using your ironing board as a buffet table.

Your turkey platter is an old hubcap.

Your best dishes have Dixie printed on them.

Your stuffing's secret ingredient comes from the bait shop.

Your only condiment on the dining room table is ketchup.

Side dishes include beef jerky and moon pies.

You have to go outside to get something out of the fridge.

The directions to your house include "turn off the paved road."

You have an Elvis Jell-O mold.

Your secret family recipe is illegal.

You serve Vienna sausage as an appetizer.

BLOOPER

The church office will be closed until opening. It will remain closed after being opened. We will be open tomorrow.

QUOTE

You can't depend on your eyes when your imagination is out of focus.

Why it's great to be a dog:

No one expects you to take a bath every day.

If it itches, you can scratch it.

There's no such thing as bad food.

A rawhide bone can entertain you for hours.

If you grow hair in weird places, no one notices.

You can lie around all day without worrying about being fired.

You don't get in trouble for putting your head in a stranger's lap.

You're always excited to see the same people.

Having big feet is considered an asset.

Puppy love can last.

BLOOPER

The church board of elders called a special meeting after church on the 15th to decide what it did last week.

QUOTE

Nothing needs reforming as much as other people's habits.

· DAY ·
64

In a small rural community, there was a Baptist church whose pastor had to double up as the local barber to make ends meet. A man living in this community had invested wisely and was enjoying his newfound comfort. One day he looked in the mirror as he was about to shave and said to himself, "I make enough money now that I don't have to shave myself. I'll go down to the barber and let him shave me from now on."

He walked into the barbershop and found that the preacher/barber was out calling on shut-ins. The barber's wife, Grace, said, "I usually do the shaves anyway. Sit down and I'll shave you." So he did.

She shaved him and he asked, "How much do I owe you?"

"Twenty-five dollars," Grace replied. The man thought that was somewhat expensive and that he might have to get a shave every other day. Nonetheless, he paid Grace and went on his way.

The next day, he woke up and found his face to be just as smooth as the day before. *No need for a shave today*, he thought. *Well, it was a twenty-five-dollar shave.*

The next day he awoke to find his face as smooth as a baby's bottom. It amazed him, as he normally would need to shave daily to keep his clean business look.

On the third day, he woke up and his face was still as smooth as the minute after Grace had finished. Now perplexed, the man went down to the barbershop to see if anyone could explain the . . . miracle.

That day the pastor was in, and the man asked him why his face was as smooth as it was that first day.

The kind old pastor gently explained, "Friend, you were shaved by Grace, and once shaved, always shaved."

BLOOPER

The celebration was a much-needed change for our church. We haven't heard laughing like that since Pastor Sears passed away.

QUOTE

The five stages of acquisition: infatuation, justification, appropriation, obsession, and resale.

I decided to visit my brother, who was stationed in Germany. I assumed that most Germans would speak English. But I found that many people spoke only their native tongue—including the ticket inspector on the train.

He punched my ticket, then chatted cordially for a bit, making gestures like a windmill. I simply nodded from time to time to show him that I was interested.

When he had gone, an American woman in the compartment leaned forward and asked if I spoke German.

"No," I confessed.

"Then that explains," she said, "why you didn't bat an eyelid when he told you that you were on the wrong train."

BLOOPER

Mark your calendars for July 12. Our annual church picnic will begin at Panfish Park at noon. In case of rain, meet at 10 under the tarp by the bandstand.

QUOTE

What's the difference between a taxidermist and a tax collector? The taxidermist only takes your skin.

Mr. Gable had a leak in the roof over his dining room, so he called a repairman to take a look at it.

"When did you first notice the leak?" the repairman asked.

Mr. Gable scowled. "Last night, when it took me two hours to finish my soup!"

BLOOPER

The church library is offering free kid rentals—hundreds of great ones to choose from.

QUOTE

A clever man commits no minor blunders.—*Goethe*

67

When we moved cross-country, my wife and I decided to drive both of our cars. Nathan, our eight-year-old, worriedly asked, "How will we keep from getting separated?"

"We'll drive slowly so that one car can follow the other," I reassured him.

"Yeah, but what if we *do* get separated?" he persisted.

"Well, then I guess we'll never see each other again," I quipped.

"Okay," he said. "Then I'm riding with Mom."

BLOOPER

Due to the lack of participation, the voluntary clean-up day at St. Mark's is now mandatory.

QUOTE

God is clever, not dishonest.—*Albert Einstein*

68

Punny truisms:

I wondered why the baseball was getting bigger. Then it hit me.

Police were called to a day care where a three-year-old was resisting a rest.

Did you hear about the guy whose whole left side was cut off? He's all right now.

The roundest knight at King Arthur's Round Table was Sir Cumference.

To write with a broken pencil is pointless.

When fish are in schools, they sometimes take debate.

The short fortune-teller who escaped from prison was a small medium at large.

A thief who stole a calendar got twelve months.

A thief fell and broke his leg in wet cement. He became a hardened criminal.

Thieves who steal corn from a garden could be charged with stalking.

We'll never run out of math teachers because they always multiply.

When the smog lifts in Los Angeles, UCLA.

The math professor went crazy with the blackboard. He did a number on it.

BLOOPER

Red tape at the Brownsville city hall is holding up our new sanctuary.

QUOTE

Here's a rule of thumb: Too clever is dumb.—*Ogden Nash*

·DAY·
69

Nancy decided to introduce her elderly mother to the magic of the internet. Her first move was to access a popular search engine, and Nancy told her mother it could answer any question she had. Nancy's mother was very skeptical, but Nancy said, "It's true, Mom. Think of something to ask it."

As Nancy sat with fingers poised over the keyboard, her mother thought a minute, then asked, "How is my sister Helen feeling?"

BLOOPER

Church member Pat Hoffman accused the chairman of the deacon board of being impartial.

QUOTE

If you have an important point to make, don't be subtle or clever. Use a pile driver. Hit the point once. Then come back and hit it again. Then hit it a third time—a tremendous whack.
—*Winston Churchill*

·DAY·
70

A taxpayer received a strongly worded "second notice" that his taxes were overdue. Hastening to the collector's office, he paid his bill, saying apologetically that he had overlooked the first notice.

"Oh," the collector said with a smile, "we don't send out first notices. We have found that the second notices are more effective."

BLOOPER

All participants in the Christmas pageant must meet at the church this Wednesday for a stress rehearsal.

QUOTE

One of the lessons of history is that nothing is often a good thing to do and always a clever thing to say.
—*Will Durant*

DAY 71

Things Mom would never say:

"How on earth can you see the TV sitting so far back?"

"Yeah, I used to skip school a lot too."

"Just leave all the lights on. It makes the house look more cheery."

"Let me smell that shirt—yeah, it's good for another week."

"Go ahead and keep that stray dog, honey. I'll be glad to feed and walk him every day."

"Well, if Timmy's mom says it's okay, that's good enough for me."

"The curfew is just a general time to shoot for. It's not like I'm running a prison around here."

"I don't have a tissue with me. Just use your sleeve."

"Don't bother wearing a jacket—the windchill is bound to improve."

BLOOPER

Last night, a car crashed into the No More Walls Family Worship Center. No injuries were reported.

QUOTE

The world does not come to the clever. It comes to the stubborn, obstinate, one-idea-at-a-time people.

DAY 72

Morris, a tourist, once came to Israel with the intention of visiting the Kotel (the Western Wall), but he forgot what it was called.

When he stepped into a taxi, he said to the driver, "Can you please take me to the place where all the Jews go to cry? Do you know where this is?"

"Sure. I'll take you there," the taxi driver answered.

He drove Morris straight to the taxation office.

BLOOPER

St. Patrick's is now offering a day-care service. Free torturing is available.

QUOTE

The world is not wanting for clever or talented or well-meaning men. It wants for men of courage and resolution.

A seafood restaurant had a sign in the window that read, "Big Lobster Tales, $5 each."

Amazed at the great value, a man stopped in and asked the waitress, "Five dollars each for lobster tails—is that correct?"

"Yes," she said. "It's our special just for today."

"Well," he said, "they must be little lobster tails."

"No," she replied, "it's the really big lobster."

"Are you sure they aren't green lobster tails—and a little bit tough?"

"No," she said, "it's the really big red lobster."

"Big red lobster tails, five dollars each?" he said, amazed. "They must be old lobster tails!"

"No, they're definitely today's," she insisted.

"Well, here's my five dollars," he said. "I'll take one."

She took the money and led him to a table, where she invited him to sit down. She then sat down next to him, leaned close, and said, "Once upon a time there was a really big red lobster . . ."

BLOOPER

Our Easter service is always well attended. We advise you to get to church early so you can get a seat in the back.

QUOTE

To be clever enough to get all that money, one must be stupid enough to want it.—*G. K. Chesterton*

DAY 74

Short Q & A:

Why does a flamingo lift up just one leg?
Because if he lifted up both legs, he would fall over!

Who invented fractions?
Henry the Eighth!

What does *minimum* mean?
A very small mother!

What does *maximum* mean?
A very big mother!

Why did Robin Hood steal from the rich?
Because the poor have nothing worth taking!

What is a skeleton?
Bones, with the person off!

BLOOPER

Everyone who attended Western Night, Pastor Haines said, had a good time, whether they liked it or not.

QUOTE

Always forgive your enemies. Nothing annoys them quite so much.—*Oscar Wilde*

DAY 75

We at the Johnson City School District have employed a new voice-mail system and would like parents to have knowledge of how it operates. When you need to reach the school, please dial the number provided. You will then have a menu of options to meet your needs.
The options are:

To lie about why your child is absent, press 1.

To make excuses for why your child did not do his work, press 2.

To complain about what we do, press 3.

To fuss at a staff member, press 4.

To ask why you didn't get needed information that was in your newsletter and several bulletins mailed to you, press 5.

If you want us to raise your child, press 6.

If you want to reach out and touch, slap, or hit someone, press 7.

If you really have an emergency, dial 911 because all these other lines will be busy.

BLOOPER	**QUOTE**
Pastor Ball said it was a once-in-a-lifetime experience, and those "only happen every so often."	I told my psychiatrist that everyone hates me. He said I was being ridiculous—everyone hasn't met me. *—Rodney Dangerfield*

· DAY ·
76

Outside a pharmacy in a busy street, a man is clutching a pole for dear life, not breathing, not moving, not twitching a muscle—just standing there, frozen.

The pharmacist, seeing this strange sight in front of his shop, goes up to his assistant and asks, "What's the matter with that guy? Wasn't he in here earlier?"

"Yes, he was," the assistant replies. "He had the most terrible cough, and none of my prescriptions seemed to help."

"He seems to be fine now."

"Sure he does," the assistant says. "I gave him a box of the strongest laxatives on the market. Now he won't dare cough!"

BLOOPER	**QUOTE**
For those still alive at the end of the service, please join us in our closing hymn.	You've got to be honest. If you can fake that, you've got it made.—*George Burns*

·DAY·
77

Two old guys are pushing their carts around Walmart when they collide. The first guy says to the second, "Sorry about that. I'm looking for my wife, and I guess I wasn't paying attention to where I was going."

The second guy says, "That's OK. And what a coincidence! I'm looking for my wife too. I can't find her and I'm getting a little desperate."

The first old guy says, "Well, maybe I can help you find her. What does she look like?"

The second old guy says, "Well, she's twenty-seven years old, tall, with red hair, blue eyes, long legs, and short shorts. What does your wife look like?"

To which the first old guy says, "Don't remember, let's look for yours."

BLOOPER

Free to good home: two great dames.

QUOTE

The difference between fiction and reality? Fiction has to make sense.
—*Tom Clancy*

·DAY·
78

"Mommy, my turtle's dead," Andrew sorrowfully told his mother, holding the turtle out to her.

His mother kissed him on the head and said, "That's all right. We'll wrap him in tissue paper, put him in a little box, and then have a nice burial ceremony in the backyard. After that, we'll go out for an ice cream cone and get you a new pet."

"Ice cream?" the little boy said, wiping his tears and smiling. Ice cream was a rare treat for him. "Oh, wow, that's great!"

His mother said, "I don't want you to be concerned . . ." Her voice trailed off as she noticed the turtle move. "Andrew, your turtle isn't dead after all!"

Andrew looked down at the turtle. "Oh," he said. He thought for a long moment, then asked in a small, hopeful voice, "Can I kill it?"

BLOOPER

At our annual church rummage sale, there will be lots of furniture—both antique and temporary.

QUOTE

I'm not afraid to die. I just don't want to be there when it happens.—*Woody Allen*

A guy is driving around and sees a sign in front of a house: "Talking Dog for Sale."

He rings the bell, and the owner tells him the dog is in the backyard. The guy goes into the backyard and sees a Labrador retriever.

"You talk?" he asks.

"Yep," the Lab replies.

"So, what's your story?"

"Well, I discovered that I could talk when I was pretty young," the Lab says. "I wanted to help the government, so I told the CIA about my gift, and in no time at all they had me jetting from country to country, sitting in rooms with spies and world leaders. I was one of their most valuable spies for eight years running.

"But jetting around really tired me out, and I knew I wasn't getting any younger, so I wanted to settle down. I signed up for a job at the airport to do some undercover security work, mostly wandering near suspicious characters and listening in. I uncovered some shady deals, and the mayor and the governor gave me a batch of medals. Then I got married, I had a mess of puppies, and now I'm just retired."

The guy is amazed. He goes back in and asks the owner what he wants for the dog.

"Ten dollars."

"This dog is amazing," the guy says. "Why on earth are you selling him so cheap?"

"Because he's a liar. He didn't do any of that stuff!"

BLOOPER

The deacon board has decided to meet this Wednesday to discuss when they should meet next.

QUOTE

Women speak because they wish to speak. Whereas a man speaks only when driven to speech by something outside himself—like, for instance, when he can't find any clean socks.

—*Jean Kerr*

DAY 80

"Cash, check, or charge?" the clerk asked after folding the items a customer wished to purchase. As the customer fumbled for her wallet, the clerk noticed a remote control for a television in her purse. "Do you always carry your TV remote?" she asked.

"No," the customer replied, "but my husband refused to come shopping with me, so I figured this was the most legal evil thing I could do to him."

BLOOPER

The Sunday school Easter egg hunt will be held behind the church from 10:00 to 10:03. Don't be late or your child may miss the excitement.

QUOTE

The pen is mightier than the sword, and considerably easier to write with.

DAY 81

One year, Johnny's parents were having a Fourth of July cookout for their extended family at their home. One of the special treats that year was lighting the fireworks they had bought out of state—since every one of them was illegal in the state they lived in. As they set up for the cookout, a cousin called, saying his neighbors' plans had just fallen through and asking if he could bring them along to the picnic. "They have a lot of food," he said.

"Sure, the more the merrier!"

When the cousin arrived with his neighbors, Johnny's family soon learned that the dad was a police officer. Johnny's father turned as innocently as he could to his son and whispered to him to grab the paper bag of fireworks sitting in the kitchen and quickly hide them somewhere. Johnny disappeared, and his father changed the topic to food for the day. The neighbor family had brought some chicken to grill, so the father told them the gas grill was all set to use out back—they just had to turn on the gas and push the ignition button with the lid still closed.

They headed out to the back as Johnny returned through the front door. His father hurried to him and said, "Whew, that was close! That man's a police officer, and he almost saw the fireworks. Did you hide them real well?"

"Oh, yeah, nobody will ever think to look in the grill!"

Church bulletin board—For sale: Yukerlaylee. And a 10-string guitar.

History will be kind to me—for I intend to write it.—*Winston Churchill*

·DAY·
82

Modern laws and principles:

You will run to answer the telephone just as the party hangs up on you. (Principle of Dingaling)

If there are only two programs on TV that are worth your time, they will always be on at the same time. (Law of Wasteland)

The cost is always higher than you budget for, and it is exactly 3.14 times higher, hence the importance of pi. (Law of Pi Eyed)

The probability that you will spill food on your clothes is directly proportional to the need to be clean. (Law of Campbell Scoop)

Each and every body submerged in a bathtub will cause the phone to ring. (Law of Yes Now)

Wind velocity will increase proportionally to the cost of your hairdo. (The Don King Principle)

After discarding something not used for years, you will need it one week later. (Law of Fatal Irreversibility)

Arriving early for an appointment will cause the receptionist to be absent, and if you arrive late, everyone else will have arrived before you. (Law of Delay)

Do not take life too seriously, because in the end, you won't come out alive anyway. (Theory of Absolute Certainty)

Our Overeaters Anonymous group has found a new meeting place. They will now meet at the Spa Creek Center, 35 Milkshake Lane.

As of yet, Bernard Shaw hasn't become prominent enough to have any enemies, but none of his friends like him.—*Oscar Wilde*

· DAY ·
83

A truck driver was traveling down the freeway and saw a sign that said "Low Bridge Ahead." Before he knew it, the bridge was directly ahead of him and he got his truck wedged under it. Cars were backed up for miles.

Finally, a police car arrived. The cop got out of his car and walked around to the truck driver, put his hands on his hips, and said, "Got stuck, huh?"

The truck driver replied, "No, I was delivering this bridge and ran out of gas."

BLOOPER

We must be kind to strangers because we may be entertaining angels in their underwear.

QUOTE

If it's the Psychic Network, why does it need a phone number?

· DAY ·
84

Once there was a little boy who lived in the country and had to use an outhouse. The little boy hated it because it was hot in the summer and cold in the winter, and it stank all the time.

The outhouse was sitting on the bank of a creek, and the boy determined that one day he would push that outhouse into the water. One day after a spring rain, the creek was swollen, so the little boy decided that today was the day. He got a large stick and pushed, and finally, the outhouse toppled into the creek and floated away.

That evening his dad sternly told him to sit down. Knowing he was in trouble, the little boy asked why. The dad replied, "Someone pushed the outhouse into the creek today. It was you, wasn't it, son?"

The boy nodded meekly. Then he thought a moment and said, "Dad, I read in school that George Washington chopped down a cherry tree and didn't get into trouble because he told the truth."

"Well, son," the dad said, "George Washington's father wasn't in that cherry tree!"

BLOOPER

Our banquet for the church's graduating seniors will feature a live prime rib and turkey carving station.

QUOTE

USA Today came out with a new survey. Apparently three out of four people make up 75 percent of the population.

A man and his wife are dining at a table in a plush restaurant, and the husband keeps staring at a drunken lady swigging her gin as she sits alone at a nearby table.

"Do you know her?" the wife asks.

"Yes," the husband says. "She's my ex-wife. She took to drinking right after we divorced seven years ago, and I hear she hasn't been sober since."

"My goodness!" the wife says. "Who would think a person could go on celebrating that long?"

BLOOPER

Church bulletin board—For sale: Alaska/hussy mixed dog.

QUOTE

Statistics on mental health state that one out of four people is suffering from some sort of mental illness. Think of three of your friends. If they are okay—then it's you.

Entry in the monthly log book of a major American corporation:

All Targets Met

All Systems Working

All Customers Satisfied

All Staff Eager and Enthusiastic

All Pigs Fed and Ready to Fly

BLOOPER

The Gary Street youth group is planning a bowel-a-thon as a fund-raiser.

QUOTE

The trouble with political jokes is that they often get elected.—*Will Rogers*

· DAY ·
87

A Jewish grandma and her grandson are at the beach. He's playing in the water and she's standing on the shore not wanting to get her feet wet. All of a sudden a huge wave appears from nowhere and crashes directly onto the spot where the boy is wading.

The water recedes and the boy is no longer there. He's been swept away.

She raises her hands to the sky as she cries, "Lord, how could you? Haven't I been a wonderful grandmother? Haven't I been a wonderful mother? Haven't I kept a kosher home? Haven't I given to B'nai B'rith? Haven't I given to Hadassah? Haven't I lit candles every Friday night? Haven't I tried my very best to live a life that you would be proud of?"

A voice booms from the sky, "Okay, okay!"

A few minutes later, another huge wave appears out of nowhere and crashes on the beach. As the water recedes, the boy is standing there, smiling and splashing around as if nothing had ever happened.

The voice booms again. "I have returned your grandson. Are you satisfied?"

She responds, "He had a hat."

BLOOPER

The Seventh Street Seniors will tour city morgue, eat ribs this Friday.

QUOTE

To love oneself is the beginning of a lifelong romance.

· DAY ·
88

Standing on the tee of a relatively long par three, an overly confident golfer said to his caddy, "Looks like a 4-wood and a putt to me."

The caddy politely disagreed and suggested that he play it safe and hit a 4-iron then a wedge. The golfer was insulted and proceeded to pout and snarl at the caddy, telling him that he was a better golfer than that, and how dare the caddy underestimate his game.

Shaken by the outburst, the caddy handed the gentleman the 4-wood he had asked for. The golfer proceeded to top the ball and watched as it rolled about fifteen yards off the front of the tee.

Coolly the caddy pulled the putter out of the bag and handed it to the golfer, saying, "And now for one long putt."

BLOOPER

Mary Carter, longtime disability advocate, will speak for the hard of hearing.

QUOTE

Copying from a single source is called plagiarism. Copying from many sources is called research.

·DAY·
89

Arnold and his wife were cleaning out the attic one day when he came across a ticket from the local shoe repair shop. The date stamped on the ticket showed it was over eleven years old. They both laughed and tried to remember which of them might have forgotten to pick up a pair of shoes over a decade ago.

"Do you think the shoes will still be in the shop?" Arnold asked.

"Not very likely," his wife said.

"It's worth a try," Arnold said, pocketing the ticket. He went downstairs, hopped into the car, and drove to the store.

With a straight face, he handed the ticket to the man behind the counter. With a face just as serious, the man said, "Just a minute. I'll have to look for these." He disappeared into a dark corner at the back of the shop.

Two minutes later, the man called out, "Here they are!"

"No kidding?" Arnold called back. "That's terrific! Who would have thought they'd still be here after all this time?"

The man came back to the counter, empty-handed.

"They'll be ready Thursday," he said.

BLOOPER

Sermon title: "If We Don't Change, Then We'll Remain the Same."

QUOTE

Always forgive your enemies, but never forget their names.

· DAY ·
90

While I was dining out with my children, a man came over to our table, and we started talking. He asked where my kids go to school. I told him we home-schooled them.

With a raised eyebrow, he asked if my husband was the sole breadwinner for our family. I said, "No, I also work, out of our home."

Then, noticing our two-month-old son, he mentioned that his daughter had just had a baby, and he wondered what hospital our son was born in.

"He was born at home," I answered.

The man looked at me and said, "Wow, you don't get out much, do you?"

BLOOPER

Church bulletin board—For sale: Electric wheelchair with patient.

QUOTE

Two things are infinite: the universe and human foolishness. I'm not sure about the universe.

· DAY ·
91

Ducking into confession with a turkey in his arms, Brian said, "Forgive me, Father, for I have sinned. I stole this turkey to feed my family. Would you take it and settle my guilt?"

"Certainly not," the priest said. "I cannot take stolen property. But as penance, you must return it to the one from whom you stole it."

"I tried," Brian sobbed. "I really have tried, but the person flatly refused to take it. Oh, Father, what should I do?"

"If what you say is true, then it is all right for you to keep it for your family."

Thanking the priest, Brian hurried off.

When confession was over, the priest returned to his residence. When he walked into the kitchen, he found that someone had stolen his turkey.

BLOOPER

Free to good home: Two cats—one black and white, the other white and black.

QUOTE

Money can't buy you happiness—but it does bring you a more pleasant form of misery.

From a passenger ship, everyone could see a bearded man on a small island, shouting and desperately waving his hands.

"Who is that man, and why is he so upset?" a passenger asked the ship's captain.

"I have no idea," the captain said, "but every year when we pass by here, he just goes crazy."

BLOOPER

Church bulletin board—For sale: Exercise bike, fully motorized.

QUOTE

A lawyer with a briefcase can steal more than a hundred men with guns.

A reporter interviewed a 104-year-old woman and asked, "What do you think is the best thing about being 104?"

She replied, "No peer pressure."

BLOOPER

Church bulletin board—For sale: GE range, $100. Dead mouse in insulation.

QUOTE

Nothing shows a man's character more than what he laughs at.

Everyone watched the beautiful bride as her father escorted her down the aisle. They reached the altar and the waiting groom. The bride kissed her father and placed something in his hand.

The minister and the guests in the front pews responded with ripples of laughter. As her father gave her away in marriage, the bride gave him back his credit card.

BLOOPER

Study shows area Christian schools inprove in some subject.

QUOTE

Pressure makes diamonds.

95

A cowboy went to an insurance agency to buy a policy. The agent asked, "Have you ever had an accident?"

"Nope," the cowboy said.

"Ever been in the hospital?"

The cowboy thought for a minute and replied, "Last summer, a bronco kicked in two of my ribs, and a couple of years ago, a rattlesnake bit me on the ankle."

The insurance agent looked surprised. "Wouldn't you call those accidents?" he asked.

"Naw," the cowboy replied. "Near as I can tell, they both did it on purpose!"

BLOOPER

QUOTE

Lost: Roscoe, Bill Kenner's black-and-white search-and-rescue dog. Last seen in front of his house.

You never lose by loving. You lose by holding back.

96

This is so funny that it will boggle your mind, and you will keep trying it several times to see if you can outsmart your foot—but you can't!

1. While sitting at your desk, lift your right foot off the floor and make clockwise circles with it.
2. Now, while doing this, draw the number "6" in the air with your right hand. Your foot will change direction!

Told you so—and there's nothing you can do about it!

·DAY· 97

Proud and pleased as she could be, the new young bride, Mrs. Stanford Strothers, strode briskly up to the teller at the bank to cash her husband's paycheck for the first time.

When the teller told her the check would have to be endorsed, the bride grabbed the pen and unhesitatingly wrote on the back, "I heartily recommend my husband, Stanford Strothers."

·DAY· 98

Heathcliffe observed a sign in the window of a restaurant that said "Unique Breakfast," so he walked in and sat down. The waitress brought him his coffee and asked him what he wanted.

"What's your unique breakfast?" Heathcliffe asked.

"Baked tongue of chicken," she replied.

"Baked tongue of chicken? Baked tongue of chicken! Do you have any idea how disgusting that is? I would never even consider eating anything that came out of a chicken's mouth!" he fumed.

Undaunted, the waitress asked, "What would you like then?"

Heathcliffe replied, "Just bring me some scrambled eggs."

DAY 99

A real estate agent had just closed his first deal only to discover that the piece of land he had sold was completely underwater.

"That customer's going to come back here pretty mad," he said to his boss. "Should I give him his money back?"

"Money back?" the boss roared. "What kind of salesman are you? Get out there and sell him a houseboat!"

BLOOPER

Church bulletin board—lost pet: Small cat. Deaf. Answers to Johnson.

QUOTE

If you try to fail and succeed, then what have you done?

DAY 100

Best college advice for incoming freshmen:

Don't LOOK at anything in a physics lab.

Don't TASTE anything in a chemistry lab.

Don't SMELL anything in a biology lab.

Don't TOUCH anything in a medical lab.

And, most importantly,

Don't LISTEN to anything in a philosophy department.

BLOOPER

Sermon title: "Life the Good Life."

QUOTE

Solitude is worse than darkness.

A wife and husband both talked in their sleep. She loved auctions; his hobby was golf.

The other night, during a deep sleep, the man yelled, "Fore!"

His wife, also in a deep sleep and not missing a beat, yelled back, "Four fifty!"

BLOOPER

Dave Horten, owner of Horten's Nursery, is offering a half-price discount on six-foot trees for Mother's Day. "Plant a tree for your mother before you have to plant your mother."

QUOTE

Flying is simple—you just aim at the ground and miss.

Just before the funeral services, the undertaker came up to the very elderly widow and asked, "How old was your husband?"

"Ninety-eight," she replied. "Two years older than I am."

"So you're ninety-six," the undertaker said.

She responded, "Hardly worth going home, is it?"

BLOOPER

Church councilman Edgers said of the building campaign, "It's a step in the right direction, but it's not a big enough step, and it's not entirely in the right direction."

QUOTE

Greta said that the secret to a long marriage was to talk every day and to keep loaded guns under lock and key.

103

Will Rogers, who died in a plane crash with Wylie Post in 1935, was probably the greatest political sage this country has ever known. Enjoy the following quotes from him:

> There are two theories to arguing with a woman. Neither works.
>
> Never miss a good chance to shut up.
>
> If you find yourself in a hole, stop digging.
>
> The quickest way to double your money is to fold it and put it back in your pocket.
>
> There are three kinds of men: ones who learn by reading, few who learn by observation, and the rest of them who have to grab the electric fence and find out for themselves.
>
> Good judgment comes from experience, and a lot of that comes from bad judgment.
>
> If you're riding ahead of the herd, take a look back every now and then to make sure it's still there.
>
> Lettin' the cat outta the bag is a whole lot easier 'n puttin' it back.
>
> After eating an entire bull, a mountain lion felt so good he started roaring. He kept it up until a hunter came along and shot him. The moral: when you're full of bull, keep your mouth shut.

BLOOPER

St. Francis Christian School students are headed to Kentucky to study the ocean.

QUOTE

I'm not bald. I'm just taller than my hair.

104

Bored during a long flight, an eminent scholar with multiple degrees in everything leaned over and woke up the sleeping man next to him to ask if he would like to play a game.

"I'll ask you a question," the scholar explained, "and if you don't know the answer, you pay me five dollars. Then you ask me a question, and if I don't know the answer, I'll pay you fifty dollars."

When the man agreed to play, the scholar asked, "What's the distance from the earth to the moon?" Flummoxed, the man handed him five dollars. "Ha!" the scholar said. "It's 238,857 miles. Now it's your turn."

The man was silent for a few moments. Then he asked, "What goes up a hill with three legs and comes down with four?"

Puzzled, the scholar racked his brain for an hour—but to no avail. Finally, he took out his wallet and handed over the fifty dollars. "Okay, okay, what's the answer?" the scholar asked.

The man said, "I don't know," pulled out a five-dollar bill, handed it to the scholar, and went back to sleep.

BLOOPER

Children's minister director Langston: "Child need some reading specialists."

QUOTE

I am not young enough to know everything.—*Oscar Wilde*

· DAY ·
105

Hang on to any of the new state of Alabama quarters. If you have them, they may be worth much more than twenty-five cents.

"We are recalling all the new Alabama quarters that were recently issued," Treasury Undersecretary Jack Shackleford said. "This action is being taken after numerous reports that the new quarters will not work in parking meters, toll booths, vending machines, pay phones, or other coin-operated devices."

The quarters were issued in the order in which the various states joined the United States and have been a tremendous success among coin collectors worldwide.

"The problem lies in the unique design of the Alabama quarter, which was created by an Auburn University graduate," Shackleford said. "Apparently, the duct tape holding the two dimes and the nickel together keeps jamming the coin-operated devices."

BLOOPER

A church headquarters audit study revealed that compulsive gamblers most often misused church funds.

QUOTE

I never think of the future. It comes fast enough.—*Albert Einstein*

DAY 106

Winters were fierce where an estate owner lived, so he felt he was doing a good deed when he bought earmuffs for his foreman. Noticing, however, that the foreman wasn't wearing the earmuffs even on the bitterest day, the landlord asked, "Didn't you like the muffs?"

"They're a thing of beauty," the foreman said.

"Then why don't you wear them?"

The foreman explained, "I was wearing them the first day, and somebody offered to buy me lunch, but I didn't hear him! Never again, never again!"

BLOOPER

Speaking to the singles' class, Vivian Moore asked that her last name not be used.

QUOTE

Imagination is everything. It is life's preview of the coming attractions.

DAY 107

A cowboy walked into a blacksmith shop and picked up a horseshoe, not realizing that it had just come from the forge. He immediately dropped it and jammed his hand into his pocket, trying to act as if nothing had happened.

The blacksmith noticed and asked with a grin, "Kind of hot, wasn't it?"

"Nope," the cowboy answered through clenched teeth. "It just doesn't take me long to look at a horseshoe."

BLOOPER

Senior supper at St. Agnes will feature pasta with garden-fresh meatballs.

QUOTE

Don't be so humble. You're not that great.—*Golda Meir*

My memory's not as sharp as it used to be. Also, my memory's not as sharp as it used to be.

But don't let aging get you down. It's too hard to get back up.

BLOOPER

Maintenance chairman Pat Stevens said that the church has purchased smoke alarms with silencers built in. "No one wants those alarms going off on Sunday morning and disturbing the service."

QUOTE

The brain is a wonderful organ. It starts working the moment you get up and does not stop until you get into the office.

A state trooper pulls a car over on a lonely back road and approaches the frazzled driver. "Ma'am, is there a reason that you're weaving all over the road?"

"Oh, officer, thank goodness you're here!" the woman replied. "I almost had an accident. I looked up and there was a tree right in front of me. I swerved to the left and there was another tree in front of me. I swerved to the right and there was another tree in front of me!"

Reaching through the side window to the rearview mirror, the officer replied, "Ma'am, that's your air freshener."

BLOOPER

Refreshments at the seniors' dinner and dance included both regular and park lemonade.

QUOTE

People love chopping wood. In this activity, one sees immediate results.

110 Two-line humor:

What would you get if you crossed a dog with a Valentine card?
A card that says, "I love you drool-ly!"

What did the painter say to her boyfriend?
"I love you with all my art!"

What does a man who loves his car do on February 14?
He gives it a Valenshine.

What did the man with the broken leg say to his nurse?
"I've got a crutch on you!"

Did you hear about the romance in the tropical fish tank?
It was a case of guppy love.

What do you call two birds in love?
Tweethearts!

What do you call a very small Valentine?
A Valentiny!

What did Frankenstein say to his girlfriend?
"Be my Valenstein!"

BLOOPER

Vickie Glassman said her aerobics and gym classes, now held at church, will also be offered online.

QUOTE

If it's true that girls are inclined to marry men like their fathers, it's understandable why so many mothers cry so much at weddings.

111 An English professor wrote the words "Woman without her man is nothing" on the blackboard and directed the students to punctuate it correctly.
The men wrote, "Woman, without her man, is nothing."
The women wrote, "Woman! Without her, man is nothing."

BLOOPER

Church bulletin board—For sale: 2004 Cadillac Sudan, all extras.

QUOTE

Intellectuals solve problems; geniuses prevent them.

DAY 112

A woman in our diet club was lamenting that she had gained weight. She'd made her family's favorite cake over the weekend, she reported, and they'd eaten half of it at dinner. The next day, she said, she kept staring at the other half, until finally she cut a thin slice for herself. One slice led to another, and soon the whole cake was gone.

The woman went on to tell us how upset she was with her lack of willpower, and how she knew her husband would be disappointed. Everyone commiserated with her, until someone asked what her husband said when he found out.

She smiled. "He never did find out. I made another cake and ate half!"

BLOOPER

The Salt Shaker Mime Show will be held at the Barker Avenue Church on Saturday night. There will also be an interpreter for the hearing impaired.

QUOTE

I found there is only one way to look thin. Hang out with really fat people.—*Rodney Dangerfield*

DAY 113

A flight attendant was getting very annoyed by three children on the plane. They had been whining and misbehaving since takeoff, complaining that they were hungry or bored or tired or thirsty or needing to go to the bathroom or whatever else you could imagine a small child complaining about.

The attendant had had enough. The next time the children said they were bored, she told them to go play outside.

BLOOPER

The plans for the Mountain View Church of Tomorrow will be unveiled tomorrow.

QUOTE

The difference between stupidity and genius is that genius has limits.

DAY 114

An artist asked the gallery owner if anyone had shown interest in his paintings that had been on display for months.

"I have good news and bad news," the gallery owner said. "The good news is that a well-dressed gentleman came in and, in the course of the conversation, asked if most paintings increased in value after the painter had . . . well, passed on. I said that in my experience, it usually happened, and the increase in value could be substantial. So he looked around a bit more and bought fifteen of your paintings."

"Well, that is just wonderful," the artist gushed. "What could possibly be bad news about that?"

The gallery owner replied, "The buyer was your doctor."

BLOOPER

Church bulletin board—For sale: Ping ping table.

QUOTE

The bad news is that time flies. The good news is that you're the pilot.

DAY 115

Security and peace of mind were part of the reason we moved to a gated community. It felt good to be protected by a tall fence and an automatic gate with a security code. Our first night there we didn't feel like cooking, so I called a local pizza shop for a delivery.

"I'd like to order a large pepperoni pizza, please," I said, then gave him the address of our condominium.

"We'll be there in about half an hour," the kid at the other end replied. "Your gate code is still 1238, right?"

BLOOPER

The Seven Mile Baptist Bible Church senior lunch programs will no longer include lunch.

QUOTE

People often say that motivation does not last. Well, neither does bathing. That's why I recommend both daily.

DAY 116

An attorney was driving through the countryside when his car failed him. He looked under the hood and knocked a few items around with a hammer. In the process, he knocked off a gas line and got his arm soaked with gas before getting the line back on. Discouraged, he attempted to start his car. Much to his surprise it started, and he headed for the nearest town for a permanent repair. To celebrate his success, he lit up a cigarette, at which time his arm exploded into flames. He stuck his arm out the window, hoping the wind at fifty miles per hour would put it out.

He was promptly pulled over by a local constable and given a ticket. The violation: illegal use of a firearm.

BLOOPER

John Foster, enrolled in the federal government's witness protection program, will be a speaker at Men's Fraternity on Friday.

QUOTE

There is nothing wrong with curiosity—unless you're a cat.

DAY 117

I was in the waiting room of my doctor's office the other day when the doctor started yelling, "Typhoid! Tetanus! Measles!" I went up to the nurse and asked her what was going on. She told me that the doctor liked to call the shots around here.

BLOOPER

Church bulletin board—For sale: 2001 Chevy Limpala.

QUOTE

Do you know what a pessimist is? A man who thinks everyone is as nasty as he is—and hates them for it.

118

I was interviewing a jeweler for a story I was writing on giving new life to old jewelry, and I asked him to tell me about his most memorable client.

"It was a divorced woman who had me make a pair of earrings from her inscribed wedding band," he said. "One earring read, 'With all,' and the other, 'my love.' When I asked why she wanted it done that way, she answered, 'To remind me that the next time anyone says that to me, I should let it go in one ear and out the other.'"

BLOOPER

Church school superintendent Briggs claims that easier school standards will result in fewer failures.

QUOTE

Failure is the condiment that gives success its flavor.

119

Two hunters got a pilot to fly them into the far north for elk hunting. They were quite successful in their venture and bagged four big bucks. The pilot came back, as arranged, to pick them up.

They started loading their gear into the plane, including the four elk. But the pilot objected and said, "The plane can only take two of your elk; you will have to leave two behind."

They argued with him, since the year before they had shot four and the pilot had allowed them to put all aboard. The plane was the same model and capacity. Reluctantly, the pilot finally permitted them to bring all four aboard. But when they attempted to take off and leave the valley, the little plane couldn't make it, and they crashed into the wilderness.

Climbing out of the wreckage, one hunter said to the other, "Do you know where we are?"

"I think so," the other hunter replied. "I think this is about the same place we crashed last year."

BLOOPER

Annual Riverside Bible Community Freedom Celebration to be held on the grounds outside Parchman Penitentiary.

QUOTE

One of the indictments of civilizations is that happiness and intelligence are so rarely found in the same person.

·DAY·
120

Benjamin is in the midst of a long dry spell in Las Vegas. Eventually he gambles away all his money and has to borrow a quarter from another gambler just to use the men's room. He finds a stall that happens to be open and pockets the quarter.

Believing that his luck has finally changed, he puts the quarter in a slot machine and hits the jackpot. He then goes to the blackjack table and turns his modest winnings into a million dollars.

Wealthy beyond his wildest dreams, Benjamin goes on the lecture circuit, where he shares his incredible story. He tells his audiences that he will always be grateful to his benefactor, and if he ever finds the man, he will share his fortune with him.

After months of speaking, a man in the audience jumps up and says, "I'm that man. I was the one who gave you the quarter."

"Yes, I remember you well, but you aren't the one I'm looking for. I mean the guy who left the stall door open!"

BLOOPER

Pastor's task force agrees: affordable housing too expensive.

QUOTE

If you teach a man to fish, you'll never sell your fish at the market.

DAY 121

The kindergarten teacher asked the students in her class to bring something related to their families' religions to class the next day. She asked for volunteers to show the rest of the class what they had brought.

One boy came forward and said, "I am Muslim, and this is my prayer rug."

Another child came forward and said, "I am Jewish, and this is my Star of David."

Another came forward and said, "I am Catholic, and this is my rosary."

The last little boy came forward and said, "I am Southern Baptist, and this is my covered dish."

BLOOPER

Cornerstone Bible senior class urged to forget that they ever suffered with memory loss.

QUOTE

The devil has put a penalty on all things I enjoy in life. Either I suffer in health or I suffer in soul or I get fat.

DAY 122

The Pope is visiting Washington, DC, and President Bush takes him out for an afternoon on the Potomac, cruising on the presidential yacht, the *Sequoia*. They're admiring the sights when all of a sudden the Pope's zucchetto (hat) blows off his head and out into the water.

The Secret Service guys start to launch a boat, but President Bush waves them off, saying, "Wait, wait. I'll take care of this. Don't worry."

Bush steps off the yacht onto the surface of the water and walks out to the Holy Father's little hat. He picks it up, walks back to the yacht, and climbs aboard, then hands the hat to the Pope amid stunned silence.

The next morning, every major newspaper in America has the same headline: "Bush Can't Swim!"

BLOOPER

Pastor Derron is staying an extra two weeks in Phoenix. He called and said that the damp weather was hard on his sciences.

QUOTE

When you are courting a beautiful girl, an hour seems like a second. When you sit on a red-hot cinder, a second seems like an eternity. That's relativity.

Golf truisms:

If you really want to get better at golf, go back and take it up at a much earlier age.

The game of golf is 90 percent mental and 10 percent mental.

Since bad shots come in groups of three, a fourth bad shot is actually the beginning of the next group of three.

When you look up and cause an awful shot, you will always look down again at exactly the moment when you ought to start watching the ball if you ever want to see it again.

Any change works for a maximum of three holes and a minimum of not at all.

Whatever you think you're doing wrong is the one thing you're doing right.

No matter how badly you're playing, it is always possible to play worse.

When your shot has to carry over a water hazard, you can hit either one more club or two more balls.

The less skilled the player, the more likely he is to share his ideas about the golf swing.

Every time a golfer makes a birdie, he must subsequently make two triple bogeys to restore the fundamental equilibrium of the universe.

BLOOPER

St. James principal Owens kills fifth grade band.

QUOTE

The only reason we have time is so that everything does not happen at once.—*Albert Einstein*

DAY 124

A blonde walks into a bank in New York City and asks for the loan officer. She's going to Europe for two weeks and needs to borrow $5,000.

The bank officer says the bank will need some kind of security for the loan, so the blonde hands over the keys to a new Mercedes-Benz SL 500. She has the title, and everything checks out.

The bank agrees to accept the car collateral for the loan. An employee of the bank drives the Benz into the bank's underground garage and parks it there. The bank's president and its officers all enjoy a good laugh at the blonde for using a $110,000 Benz as collateral against a $5,000 loan.

Two weeks later, the blonde returns. She repays the $5,000 and the interest, which comes to $15.41.

The loan officer says, "Miss, we are happy to have had your business, and this transaction worked out very nicely, but we are a little puzzled. While you were away, we checked you out and found that you're a multimillionaire. What puzzles us is, why would you bother to borrow $5,000?"

The blonde replies, "Where else in New York City can I park my car for two weeks for only $15.41 and expect it to be there when I return?"

Finally, a smart blonde joke.

BLOOPER

We welcome all visitors to Trinity Presperation Church.

QUOTE

A man likes his wife to be just clever enough to appreciate his cleverness, and just simple enough to admire it.

While attending a marriage seminar dealing with communication, Tom and his wife, Grace, listened to the instructor say, "It is essential that husbands and wives know the things that are important to each other." He then addressed the men: "Can you describe your wife's favorite flower?"

Tom leaned over, touched his wife's arm gently, and whispered, "It's Pillsbury, isn't it?"

The rest of the story gets rather ugly, so I'll stop right here.

BLOOPER

The Riggs Bible Chapel Cemetery is making a comeback.

QUOTE

An inefficient virus kills its host. A clever virus stays with it.

A husband read an article to his wife about how many words women use a day: thirty thousand to a man's fifteen thousand. The wife said, "The reason has to be because we have to repeat everything to men."

The husband turned to his wife and asked, "What?"

BLOOPER

Christian school student survey: "4 out of 10 hate math—a majority."

QUOTE

Don't be too clever for an audience. Make it obvious. Make the subtleties obvious too.

· DAY ·
127

Once upon a time there was a prince who, through no fault of his own, was cast under a spell by an evil witch. The curse was that the prince could speak only one word each year. However, he could save up the words so that if he did not speak for a whole year, the following year he was allowed to speak two words, and so on.

One day he met a beautiful princess (ruby lips, golden hair, sapphire eyes) and fell madly in love. With the greatest difficulty he decided to refrain from speaking for two whole years so that he could look at her and say, "My darling." But at the end of the two years he wished to tell her that he loved her as well. Because of this he waited three more years without speaking.

But at the end of these five years he realized that he also wanted to ask her to marry him. So he waited another four years without speaking.

Finally, as the ninth year of silence ended, his joy knew no bounds. Leading the lovely princess to the most secluded and romantic place in the beautiful royal garden, the prince heaped a hundred red roses on her lap, knelt before her, took her hand in his, and said huskily, "My darling, I love you! Will you marry me?"

The princess tucked a strand of hair behind a dainty ear, opened her eyes in wonder, parted her lips, and said, "Pardon?"

BLOOPER

Bob Graham, elder candidate, is a Golf War veteran.

QUOTE

Educate man without religion and you make them but clever devils.—*Arthur Wellesley*

· DAY ·
128

There was an unexpected knock on my door, and like I always do, I first opened the peephole and asked, "Who's there?"

"Parcel post, ma'am. I have a package that needs a signature."

"Where's the package?" I asked. The deliveryman held it up.

"Could I see some ID?" I said, still not convinced.

"Lady," he replied wearily, "if I wanted to break into your house, I'd probably just use these." And he pulled out the keys I had left in the door.

BLOOPER

Richard King, a member of the Jennerstown Lutheran Church deacon board, said no one is accusing any of the elders of honesty.

QUOTE

He is very clever, but sometimes the brains go to his head.

·DAY·
129

I noticed the neighbor down the street was home every day, so after a few weeks I asked him what was going on. He said, "I left my job because of illness and fatigue."

A few weeks later, his wife gave me the real truth of what happened. Turns out my neighbor's boss got sick and tired of him.

BLOOPER

Missy Lopper, teaching specialist, will present a seminar to all interested church parents: "Math! It's as easy as A-B-C!"

QUOTE

I write my own quotes. Except this one. I obviously stole this one from someone really clever.

·DAY·
130

My sister was bemoaning the fact that she had procrastinated cleaning and organizing her house for a long time. Since she was planning to entertain, she felt a lot of pressure to get moving. That afternoon she phoned, sounding glum.

"I went to the bookstore," she said, "and I bought a book on how to get organized. I was all fired up, and I decided to clean out all the shelves in the living room. While I was cleaning, I found the same blasted book—I bought it a couple of years ago!"

BLOOPER

Members—take note! Please exit the new church driveway, which is the one between the old entrance and the old exit. Please exit from the new exit, which is the old exit.

QUOTE

A man who dares to waste one hour of his time has not discovered the value of life.

DAY 131

When I was:

Four years old: My daddy can do anything.

Five years old: My daddy knows a whole lot.

Eight years old: My dad doesn't know exactly everything.

Ten years old: In the olden days, when my dad grew up, things were sure different.

Twelve years old: Oh, well, naturally, Dad doesn't know anything about that. He's too old to remember his childhood.

Fourteen years old: Don't pay any attention to my dad. He is so old-fashioned.

Twenty-one years old: Him? My goodness, he's hopelessly out of date.

Twenty-five years old: Dad knows about it, but then he should, because he has been around so long.

Thirty years old: Maybe we should ask Dad what he thinks. After all, he's had a lot of experience.

Thirty-five years old: I'm not doing a single thing until I talk to Dad.

Forty years old: I wonder how Dad would have handled it. He was so wise.

Fifty years old: I'd give anything if Dad were here now so I could talk this over with him. Too bad I didn't appreciate how smart he was. I could have learned a lot from him.

BLOOPER

Ned Wiley brought his new electric car to the men's gathering—the car runs on gasoline.

QUOTE

Anyone can face a crisis. It is day-to-day living that wears you out.—*Anton Chekhov*

Top ten things a teenage daughter doesn't want to hear from her dad:

10. "Let me explain what 'deductible' means on car insurance."
 9. "Your mom's almost ready. Where are we going on our double date?"
 8. "Seems to me last year's prom dress still has some life in it."
 7. "I signed us up for the pairs karaoke contest this Friday night."
 6. "We ate possum toes like popcorn when I was a kid."
 5. "Let's get ice cream, my treat! Just let me grab my jar of coins."
 4. "I am proud that you decided to keep the family unibrow."
 3. "You don't need to go shopping after all. I picked out a purse for you on my way home."
 2. "I ran into Bobby at the grocery store. I told him that you're really hoping he'll ask you to the dance."
 1. "By the way, I had to borrow your deodorant yesterday."

BLOOPER

Pastor Yernee said that deaf people don't listen to fraud warnings.

QUOTE

Don't go around saying the world owes you a living. The world owes you nothing. It was here first.—*Mark Twain*

I had just pulled into a parking spot at the home improvement store when smoke and flames began pouring from under my hood.

Frantic, I bolted into the store and ran up to the first clerk I saw. As luck would have it, he was standing behind the customer service counter.

"Please help," I gasped. "My car's on fire! I need a fire extinguisher!"

Without even looking up, he replied, "Aisle 12."

BLOOPER

Bride Cindy Fox wore a lovely lace veil that fell to the floor as she walked down the aisle.

QUOTE

Every man dies. Not every man really lives.—*William Wallace*

·DAY·
134

I am just sitting down in the public restroom when I hear a voice from the other stall saying, "Hi, how are you?"

I don't know what gets into me, as I'm not the type to start a conversation in a men's restroom at a rest stop, but I answer, somewhat embarrassed, "Doin' just fine!"

"So what are you up to?" the other guy says.

What kind of question is that? At this point, I'm thinking this is too bizarre, so I say, "Uhhh, I'm like you, just traveling east."

Now I am just trying to get out as fast as I can, when I hear another question: "Can I come over to your place after a while?"

Okay, this question is just wacky, but I figure I can be polite and end the conversation. I tell him, "Well, I have company over, so today is a bad day for me."

Then I hear the guy say, "Listen, I'll have to call you back. There's an idiot in the other stall who keeps answering all my questions!"

BLOOPER	QUOTE
Harvest Church member Becky Heartsel wins dog show.	He who has a why to live can bear almost any how.—*Friedrich Nietzsche*

·DAY·
135

My son is a sports fanatic and has well-worn T-shirts, caps, and sweatshirts from every local team. One night, we were getting ready for an annual fund-raiser for our local theater organization.

My wife called out to my son, "This is a pretty fancy dinner. You'll have to wear a sports jacket."

My son answered, "Which team?"

BLOOPER	QUOTE
Visitation pastor Kline said that Rebecca's terminal illness did not seem too severe.	I arise in the morning torn between a desire to improve the world and a desire to enjoy the world. This makes it hard to plan the day.—*E. B. White*

How to install a wireless security system:

Go to a secondhand store and buy a pair of men's used work boots . . . a really big pair. Put them outside your front door on top of a copy of *Guns and Ammo* magazine. Put a dog dish beside it . . . a really big dish. Leave a note on your front door that says something like this: "Bubba, Big Mike, and I have gone to get more ammunition. Back in 30 minutes. Don't disturb the pit bulls—they've just been wormed."

BLOOPER

On a sign at St. Michael's Church in Herrid, South Dakota, during a frigid spell: "Many are cold, but few are chosen."

QUOTE

I have a simple philosophy: Fill what's empty. Empty what's full. Scratch where it itches.—*Alice Roosevelt Longworth*

My heart sank as I read the spam that began, "By opening this email, you have activated the Amish computer virus."

Then I realized that not only was my computer in jeopardy, so was my reputation as it continued, "Since the Amish don't have computers, this works on the honor system. Please delete all your files. Thank you."

BLOOPER

The Women's Guild suggests that you prepare for Christmas now—and get your rabies shots early.

QUOTE

I have discovered the secret of life— you just hang around until you get used to it.—*Charles M. Schulz*

·DAY·

138

Bob and his three golf buddies were out playing and were just starting on the back nine when Bob paused, looked down the fairway, and began to sob uncontrollably.

The other three gathered around him and asked, "What's wrong?"

Bob looked down at his feet, sniffed, and dried his eyes, then apologized for his emotional outburst. "I'm sorry, I always get emotional at this hole. It holds very difficult memories for me."

One of his buddies asked, "What happened? What could have gotten you so upset?"

Bob stared silently off in the distance, then said, "This is where my brother and I were playing twelve years ago when he suddenly died of a heart attack—right at this very hole!"

"Oh no!" the other golfers said. "That must have been horrible!"

"Horrible? You think it's horrible?" Bob cried in disbelief. "It was worse than that! Every hole for the rest of the day, all the way back to the clubhouse, it was hit the ball, drag Ted, hit the ball, drag Ted . . ."

BLOOPER

The church elder meeting on open meetings is closed to the church.

QUOTE

In three words I can sum up everything I've learned about life: it goes on.—*Robert Frost*

·DAY·

139

A group of friends went deer hunting and paired off in twos for the day. That night one of the hunters returned alone, staggering under the weight of a ten-point buck.

"Where's Henry?" someone asked.

"He had a stroke of some kind. He's a couple of miles back up the trail."

"You left Henry lying out there and carried the deer back?"

"A tough call," the hunter said, "but I figured no one is going to steal Henry."

BLOOPER

Dr. Serle will lead a marriage and depression seminar for all interested church members this Sunday night.

QUOTE

Use your health, even to the point of wearing it out. That is what it is for. Spend it all before you die; do not outlive yourself.—*George Bernard Shaw*

· DAY ·
140

A young man was walking through a supermarket to pick up a few things when he noticed an old lady following him around.

Thinking nothing of it, he ignored her and continued on. Finally, he went to the checkout line, but she got in front of him.

"Pardon me," she said, "I'm sorry if my staring at you has made you feel uncomfortable. It's just that you look exactly like my son who just died recently."

"I'm very sorry," the young man said. "Is there anything I can do for you?"

"Yes," she said. "As I'm leaving, can you say, 'Good-bye, Mother'? It would make me feel so much better."

"Sure," the young man answered. As the old woman was leaving, he called out, "Good-bye, Mother!"

As he stepped up to the checkout counter, he saw that his total was $127.50. "How can that be?" he asked. "I only purchased a few things!"

The clerk replied, "Your mother said you would be paying for her."

BLOOPER

The St. Barnabas youth group will once again be selling their mothwatering frozen pizzas. Please see Jeff in the lobby.

QUOTE

When I stand before God at the end of my life, I would hope that I would not have a single bit of talent left, and could say, "I used everything you gave me."—*Erma Bombeck*

DAY 141

Typoglycemia

Don't skip this because it looks weird. Believe it or not, you can read it!

I cdnuolt blveiee taht I cluod aulaclty uesdnatnrd waht I was rdanieg. The pheonmneal pweor of the hmuan mnid. . . . Aoccdrnig to a rseearch taem at Cmabrigde Uinervtisy, it deosn't mttaer in waht oredr the ltteers in a wrod are, the olny iprmoatnt tihng is taht the frist and lsat ltteer be in the rghit pclae. The rset can be a taotl mses and you can sitll raed it wouthit a porbelm. Tihs is bcuseae the huamn mnid deos not raed ervey lteter by istlef, but the wrod as a wlohe. Such a cdonition is arppopiatrely cllaed Typoglycemia.

Amzanig, huh? Yaeh, and you awlyas thguoht slpeling was ipmorantt.

BLOOPER

The Easter candies given to the elementary classes this Sunday have been certified kosher.

QUOTE

A hug is like a boomerang—you get it back right away.

DAY 142

A young clergyman, fresh out of seminary, thought it would help him better understand the fears and temptations his future congregations faced if he first took a job as a policeman for several months. He passed the physical examination, then came the oral exam to test his ability to act quickly and wisely in an emergency.

Among other questions, he was asked, "What would you do to disperse a frenzied crowd?"

He thought for a moment and then said, "I would take up a collection."

· DAY ·

143

Two sisters, one blonde and one brunette, inherit the family ranch. Unfortunately, after just a few years, they are in financial trouble and have only six hundred dollars left. To keep the bank from repossessing the ranch, they need to purchase a bull from the stockyard in a far town so they can breed their own stock. Upon leaving, the brunette tells her sister, "When I get there, if I decide to buy the bull, I'll contact you to drive out after me and haul it home."

The brunette arrives at the stockyard, inspects the bull, and decides she wants to buy it. The man tells her that he will sell it for $599, no less. After paying him, she drives to the nearest town to send her sister a telegram and tell her the news. She walks into the telegraph office and tells the operator what she needs.

The operator explains that he'll be glad to help her, then adds, "It's just ninety-nine cents a word." The brunette now has only one dollar left and realizes that she'll be able to send her sister only one word.

After a few minutes of thinking, she nods and says, "I want you to send her the word *comfortable*."

The operator shakes his head. "How is she ever going to know that you want her to hitch the trailer to your pickup truck and drive out here to haul that bull back to your ranch if you send her just the word *comfortable*?"

The brunette explains, "My sister's a blonde. The word's big. She'll read it very slowly: 'com-for-da-bull'!"

•DAY•

144

Morris, a city boy, moved to the country and bought a donkey from an old farmer for a hundred dollars. The farmer agreed to deliver the animal.

The next day, the farmer drove up and said, "Sorry, but I have some bad news. The donkey died."

"Well then, just give me my money back."

"Can't do that. I went and spent it already."

"Okay then. Just unload the donkey."

"What ya gonna do with him?"

"I'm going to raffle him off."

"You can't raffle off a dead donkey!"

"Sure I can. Watch me."

A month later the farmer met up with the city boy and asked, "Whatever happened with that dead donkey?"

"I raffled him off. I sold five hundred tickets at two dollars apiece and made a profit of $998."

"Didn't anyone complain?"

"Just the guy who won. So I gave him his two dollars back."

BLOOPER	QUOTE
Dance the night away from 6 to 8 p.m. with the Seniors with Class at Petler Hill Episcopal Church.	Love is the beauty of the soul.—*Saint Augustine*

Punny truisms:

> The professor discovered that her theory of earthquakes was on shaky ground.
>
> The dead batteries were given out free of charge.
>
> If you take a laptop computer for a run, you could jog your memory.
>
> A dentist and a manicurist fought tooth and nail.
>
> What's the definition of a will? (It's a dead giveaway.)
>
> A bicycle can't stand alone; it is two-tired.
>
> Time flies like an arrow; fruit flies like a banana.
>
> A backward poet writes inverse.
>
> In a democracy, it's your vote that counts; in feudalism, it's your count that votes.
>
> A chicken crossing the road: poultry in motion.
>
> If you don't pay your exorcist, you can get repossessed.
>
> With her marriage, she got a new name and a dress.
>
> Show me a piano falling down a mine shaft and I'll show you A-flat miner.

BLOOPER

Sarah Drake, children's ministry worker, said that obese children have a huge impact.

QUOTE

A friend is one who knows you and loves you just the same.

·DAY·

146 A woman had a beautiful black cat with white feet named Socks. Socks spent his days outside and came indoors only at night. But one cool October evening he disappeared.

She searched for him high and low for several days, but all in vain. The following spring, however, Socks reappeared, looking healthy and clean. She figured he'd just been out sowing his wild oats, and let it go at that.

Everything was back to normal until that autumn, when Socks once again disappeared. The next spring, just as in the prior year, he returned. When it happened for the third year in a row, the woman became perplexed and decided to investigate. She started by asking her neighbors to see what, if any, information they might have.

Finally she was down to the last house on the block, the home of an older couple. She went up and knocked on the door. The lady of the house answered, and Socks's owner asked her, "By any chance, have you ever seen a black cat with four white feet around here?"

"A black cat?" the woman said. "With four white feet? Oh my, yes! He's the sweetest thing. My husband and I kept seeing him outside every fall. We hated it that the poor thing had to be out in the cold, so we decided that when we go south for the winter, we'd take him with us. He's been going to Florida with us every winter for the last few years."

BLOOPER

Our local hospital, Dane County Hospital, is seeking volunteers for light cervical duties.

QUOTE

Be courteous to all, but intimate with few, and let those few be well tried before you give them your confidence.
—*George Washington*

·DAY·

147 Little Johnny wanted to go to the zoo and pestered his parents for days. Finally, his mother talked his reluctant father into taking him.

"So how was it?" his mother asked when they returned home.

"Great," little Johnny replied.

"Did you and your father have a good time?"

"Yeah, Daddy really liked it," Johnny exclaimed, "especially when one of the animals came home at 30 to 1!"

BLOOPER

Fourth Street Lutheran Church's "We Care" line has been disconnected.

QUOTE

Friendship is unnecessary, like philosophy, like art. It has no survival value; rather it is one of those things that give value to survival.—*C. S. Lewis*

·DAY·
148

In Africa, a company from Hollywood was producing an English-language movie. In one scene, an exhausted messenger was supposed to dash in, collapse, and gasp out a vital message in Swahili. It was easy to find someone who knew the language. The scene worked beautifully in the movie—until it played in an African town where Swahili was well-known. A moment of high drama nose-dived into comedy as the panting messenger gasped out, "I don't think I'm being paid enough for this part!"

BLOOPER

Owl Creek Lutheran School students picked a new mascot—an owl.

QUOTE

The bird a nest, the spider a web, man friendship.—*William Blake*

·DAY·
149

My sister and I are close, and that allows us to be honest with each other. One evening as I prepared for a date, I remarked, "I'm fat."
"No, you're not," she said.
"My hair is awful."
"It's lovely."
"I've never looked worse," I whined.
She said, "Yes, you have."

BLOOPER

Remember, Christmas is Wednesday, December 28.

QUOTE

A true friend stabs you in the front. —*Oscar Wilde*

·DAY·
150

Working at the post office, I'm used to dealing with a moody public. So when one irate customer stormed my desk, I responded in my calmest voice, "What's the trouble?"

"I went out this morning," she began, "and when I came home, I found a card saying the mailman tried to deliver a package but no one was home. I'll have you know, my husband was in all morning! He never heard a thing! Your mail carrier must be negligent."

After apologizing, I got her parcel.

"Oh good!" she gushed. "We've been waiting for this for ages!"

"What is it?" I asked.

"My husband's new hearing aid."

BLOOPER

The senior high Christmas dinner will feature elf cutlets in a butter sauce.

QUOTE

Wishing to be friends is quick work, but friendship is a slow-ripening fruit.
—*Aristotle*

·DAY·
151

The owner of a small deli was being questioned by the IRS about his tax return. He had reported a net profit of $80,000 for the year.

"Why don't you people leave me alone?" the deli owner said. "I work like a dog, everyone in my family helps out, and the place is closed only three days a year. And you want to know how I made $80,000?"

"It's not your income that bothers us," the agent said. "It's these deductions. You listed six trips to Bermuda for you and your wife."

"Oh, that," the owner said, smiling. "I forgot to tell you—we also deliver."

BLOOPER

Once again, the St. Peter's youth group is selling firewood. Pastor Dan reminds everyone to be careful—the wood is quite flammable.

QUOTE

A man begins cutting his wisdom teeth the first time he bites off more than he can chew.

A businessman on his deathbed called his friend and said, "Bill, I want you to promise me that when I die, you will have my remains cremated."

"And what," his friend asked, "do you want me to do with your ashes?"

"Just put them in an envelope and mail them to the Internal Revenue Service," the businessman said. "Write on the envelope, 'Now you have everything.'"

BLOOPER

Due to Paulette Gordon's laryngitis, the deaf awareness seminar is postponed.

QUOTE

Every man is a fool for at least five minutes a day; wisdom consists of not exceeding the limit.

After the egg hunt on Easter Sunday, a young farm boy decided to play a prank. He went to the chicken coop and replaced every single egg with a brightly colored one.

A few minutes later the rooster walked in, saw all the colored eggs, then stormed outside and beat up the peacock!

BLOOPER

Church bulletin board—For sale: Outdoor nativity scene—missing only Mary, Joseph, and Jesus.

QUOTE

Honesty is the first chapter of the book of wisdom.—*Thomas Jefferson*

DAY 154

Two bachelors were talking. One said to the other, "I got a cookbook the other day, but I can't do any of the recipes."

"Why? Are they too difficult?" the second asked.

"No," the first replied. "It's just that they all start with the same thing: 'Take a clean dish . . .'"

BLOOPER

Happy Valley Christian Senior Villa will hold its annual New Year's Eve party. The countdown begins at 12 noon and the party will last until 5 p.m.

QUOTE

Patience is the companion of wisdom.—*Saint Augustine*

DAY 155

After years of using the same perfumes, I decided to try something different and settled on a light, citrusy fragrance.

The next day I was surprised when it was my little boy, not my husband, who first noticed the change. As he put his arms around me, he declared, "Wow, Mom, you smell just like Froot Loops!"

BLOOPER

The Church Sportsman Club has set November 12 for their disabled turkey hunt.

QUOTE

Women marry men hoping they will change. Men marry women hoping they will not. So each is inevitably disappointed.

DAY 156

My husband, Ray, was attempting to build a patio for the first time and bought a hundred cement blocks. Laying them out in a pattern, he discovered the chosen area was too small.

He stacked the blocks against the house and cleared more space. The next day Ray put the cement blocks back down, only to find that the ground was too hard to keep the patio level.

He ordered a truckload of sand to be delivered the following morning. Again he stacked the hundred blocks against the house.

Observing all this, our next-door neighbor asked, "Ray, are you going to put your patio away every night?"

BLOOPER

Westmoreland County Meals on Wheels, headquartered in the basement annex of the church, will now provide pet food for seniors.

QUOTE

The more sand that has escaped through the hourglass of our life, the clearer we should see through it.

·DAY· 157

My mother was away all weekend at a business conference. During a break, she decided to call home collect. My six-year-old brother picked up the phone and heard a stranger's voice say, "We have a Betty on the line. Will you accept the charges?"

Frantic, he dropped the receiver and came charging outside, screaming, "Dad! They've got Mom! And they want money!"

BLOOPER

Call the Pine Bluff Presbyterian Church confidential hotline for a message. No one will talk to you.

QUOTE

There is a wisdom of the head and a wisdom of the heart.—*Charles Dickens*

·DAY· 158

After her son fell into the pond yet again and came home with his good school clothes dripping wet, his exasperated mother sent him to his room and washed and dried his clothes.

A little later, she heard a commotion in the backyard and called out, "Are you out there wetting your pants again?"

There was dead silence for a moment. Then a deep, masculine voice answered meekly, "No, ma'am, I'm just reading the meter."

BLOOPER

Church bulletin board: Free to a good home—Jack Russell terrorist.

QUOTE

Act as if what you do makes a difference. It does.—*William James*

·DAY·

159

Donald MacDonald, a student from the Isle of Skye in Scotland, was admitted into the prestigious Oxford University and was living in the residence hall his first year there. His clan was so excited that one of their own had made it into the upper class of education, but they were concerned how he would do in "that strange land."

After the first month, his mother came to visit. "How do you find the English students, Donald?" she asked.

"Mother," he replied in his thick brogue, "they're such terrible, noisy people. The one on that side keeps banging his head against the wall, and he won't stop. The one on the other side screams and screams and screams into the night."

"Oh, Donald! How do you manage to put up with those awful, noisy English neighbors?"

"Mother, I just ignore them. I simply stay here quietly, playing my bagpipes."

BLOOPER	QUOTE
Dr. Betty reminds the whole church that flu shots can be prevented with flu shots.	Always do your best. What you plant now, you will harvest later.—*Og Mandino*

·DAY·

160

As the manager of our hospital's softball team, I was responsible for returning equipment to the proper owners at the end of the season.

When I walked into the surgery department carrying a bat that belonged to one of the surgeons, I passed several patients and their families in a waiting area.

I heard one man say to his wife, "Look, honey, here comes your anesthesiologist."

BLOOPER

Tom Thumb Supermarkets will sponsor a prostate awareness seminar at our men's monthly meeting.

QUOTE

Be gentle to all and stern with yourself.—*Saint Teresa of Avila*

·DAY·
161

My husband and I both work, so our family eats out a lot. Recently, when we were having a rare home-cooked meal, I handed a glass to my three-year-old and asked her to please drink her milk.

She looked at me, bewildered, and said, "But I didn't order milk!"

BLOOPER

As part of the city and church task force, hat crimes are on the agenda for the upcoming meeting.

QUOTE

It is always too early to quit.—*Norman Vincent Peale*

·DAY·
162

A Polish immigrant goes to the Wisconsin Department of Motor Vehicles in Milwaukee to apply for a driver's license and is told he has to take an eye test. The examiner shows him a card with these letters:

C Z J W I X N O S T A C Z

"Can you read this?" the examiner asks.

"Read it?" the Polish guy replies. "I know the guy!"

BLOOPER

Parents' Day at St. Michael's: Discuss your child's leaning problems with his teacher.

QUOTE

Small deeds done are better than great deeds planned.—*Peter Marshall*

·DAY·

163

The teacher asked one of her young students if he knew his numbers.

"Yes," he said, "I do. My father taught me."

"Good. What comes after three?"

"Four," the boy said.

"What comes after six?"

"Seven."

"Very good," the teacher said. "Your dad did a good job. What comes after ten?"

"A jack."

BLOOPER

Church bulletin board—For sale: Texas Hold 'Em polka table, new.

QUOTE

The harder the conflict, the more glorious the triumph.—*Thomas Paine*

·DAY·

164

A guy was telling his friend that he and his wife had had a serious argument the night before. "But it ended," he said, "when she came crawling to me on her hands and knees."

"What did she say?" his friend asked.

"She said, 'Come out from under that bed, you coward!'"

BLOOPER

Banker Tom Neely spoke to our adult Sunday school group on money. He instructed the class on how to divide a dollar: 30 cents goes to savings, 30 cents should be invested, 30 cents should be allocated for current spending, and finally, 30 cents should be earmarked for church and charity.

QUOTE

To be a good loser is to learn how to win.—*Carl Sandburg*

My father is a skilled CPA who is not great at self-promotion. So when an advertising company offered to put my father's business placard in the shopping carts of a supermarket, my dad jumped at the chance. Fully a year went by before we got a call that could be traced to those placards.

"Richard Larson, CPA?" the caller asked.

"That's right," my father answered. "May I help you?"

"Yes," the voice said. "One of your shopping carts is in my yard, and I want you to come and get it."

BLOOPER

Church bulletin board: Church cookbooks are still on sale. Save $1 if you order by mail. Just add $1 for handling.

QUOTE

Wherever you are—be all there.
—*Jim Elliot*

Bob had a problem of getting up late in the morning and was always late for work. After a few weeks of this, his boss was mad and threatened to fire him if he didn't do something about it.

Bob went to his doctor, who gave him a pill and told him to take it before he went to bed. He got a great night's sleep and actually beat the alarm in the morning. After a leisurely breakfast, he drove to work.

"Boss," he said, "the pill my doctor prescribed actually worked!"

"That's fine," his boss said, "but where were you yesterday?"

BLOOPER

Church bulletin board—For sale: Buick Regal with curse control.

QUOTE

You can't build a reputation on what you are going to do.—*Henry Ford*

· DAY ·
167

Three paramedics were boasting about improvements in their respective ambulance team's response times.

"Since we installed our new satellite navigation system," the first one said, "we cut our emergency response time by 10 percent."

The other paramedics nodded in approval. "Not bad," the second paramedic commented. "But by using a computer model of traffic patterns, we've cut our average response time by 20 percent."

Again, the other team members gave their congratulations, until the third paramedic said, "That's nothing. Since our ambulance driver passed the bar exam, we've cut our emergency response time in half!"

BLOOPER

Job posting: Elderly lady would like a housepeeker.

QUOTE

Belief creates the actual fact.
—*William James*

· DAY ·
168

You know it's time to diet when:

You dance and it makes the band skip.

You are diagnosed with the flesh-eating virus, and the doctor gives you twenty-two more years to live.

You put mayonnaise on an aspirin.

You go to the zoo and the elephants throw you peanuts.

Your driver's license says, "Picture continued on other side."

You run away, and your picture takes up all four sides of the milk carton.

You could sell shade.

Your blood type is Ragu.

BLOOPER

Kids' Nite Out: Learn how to protect yourself from karate master Kevin Worts.

QUOTE

Change your thoughts and you change your world.—*Norman Vincent Peale*

A carpet installer had just finished laying carpet for a lady. He stepped out for a smoke, only to realize he'd misplaced his cigarettes.

In the middle of the room, under the carpet, was a bump.

"No sense pulling up the entire floor for one pack of smokes," he said to himself. He proceeded to get out his hammer and flattened the hump.

As he was cleaning up, the lady came in. "Here, I found them in the hallway," she said, handing him his pack of cigarettes. "Now, if only I could find my parakeet."

BLOOPER

The Sunday school superintendent told the elder board that his confidence in the public school system is laking.

QUOTE

Do not judge each day by the harvest you reap but by the seeds that you plant.—*Robert Louis Stevenson*

The teacher was giving her class of seven-year-olds a natural history lesson. "Worker ants," she told them, "can carry pieces of food five times their own weight. What do you conclude from that?"

One child was ready with the answer: "They don't have a union."

BLOOPER

Church bulletin board—For sale: 1910 Bible—family air loom.

QUOTE

Every moment and every event of every man's life on earth plants something in his soul.—*Thomas Merton*

·DAY·

171

I was a new army basic trainee at Fort McClellan, and one requirement was a demanding twelve-mile march. We got started at six a.m. and were pumped up for the trek.

An hour later, feeling the heavy load of our packs, we wondered if the end would ever come. "Men," our sergeant yelled, "you're doing a fine job. We've already covered four miles!"

Revitalized, we picked up the pace.

"And," Sarge continued, "we should reach the starting point any minute now."

BLOOPER

Victory Sports Camps will be selling assaulted peanuts to support their summer camp program.

QUOTE

Give light and people will find the way.—*Ella Baker*

·DAY·

172

Golf truisms:

A golf match is a test of your skill against your opponent's luck.

It's surprisingly easy to hole a fifty-foot putt when you lie for ten.

Counting on your opponent to inform you when he breaks a rule is like expecting him to make fun of his own haircut.

The statute of limitations on forgotten strokes is two holes.

Nonchalant putts count the same as chalant putts.

Always limp with the same leg for the whole round.

Nothing straightens out a nasty slice quicker than a sharp dogleg to the right.

The shortest distance between any two points on a golf course is a straight line that passes directly through the center of a very large tree.

It's often necessary to hit a second drive to really appreciate the first one.

You can hit a two-acre fairway 10 percent of the time, and a two-inch branch 90 percent of the time.

A stroke does not occur unless it is observed by more than one golfer.

Get involved in our community outreach. Give blood and make your own sundae this Wednesday.

God always gives his best to those who leave the choice with him.—*Jim Elliot*

·DAY·
173

The cat's New Year's resolutions:

- I will not play "Herd of Thundering Wildebeests Stampeding across the Plains of the Serengeti" over any human's bed while she's trying to sleep.
- I cannot leap through closed windows to catch birds outside. If I forget this and bonk my head on the window and fall behind the couch in my attempt, I will not get up and do the same thing again.
- I will not stick my paw into any container to see if there is something in it. And if I do, I will not hiss and scratch when my human has to shave me to get the rubber cement out of my fur.
- I will not play "dead cat on the stairs" while people are trying to bring in groceries or laundry, or else one of these days it will really come true.
- I will not swat my human's head repeatedly when he is on the family room floor trying to do sit-ups.
- I will not puff my entire body to twice its size for no reason after my human has watched a horror movie.
- I will not perch on my human's chest in the middle of the night and stare until he wakes up.
- I will not walk on the keyboard when my human is writing important adagfsg gdjagx;ln.
- If I must claw my human, I will not do it in such a way that the scars resemble a botched suicide attempt.

Church bulletin board—For sale: Pet door—8 feet tall, never used.

Gratitude is the fairest blossom which springs from the soul.—*Henry Ward Beecher*

Latest terms to add to your vocabulary at the office:

Blamestorming—Sitting around in a group discussing why a deadline was missed or a project failed and who was responsible.

Chainsaw Consultant—An outside expert brought in to reduce the employee head count, leaving the brass with clean hands.

CLM (Career-Limiting Move)—Ill-advised activity. (E.g., trashing your boss while he or she is within earshot is a serious CLM.)

Dilberted—To be exploited and oppressed by your boss. Derived from the experiences of Dilbert, the geek-in-a-cubicle comic strip character. (E.g., "I've been Dilberted again. The old man revised the specs for the fourth time this week.")

404—Someone who's clueless. From the world wide web error message "404 Not Found," meaning that the requested document could not be located. (E.g., "Don't bother asking him—he's 404, man.")

Keyboard Plaque—The disgusting buildup of dirt and crud found on computer keyboards.

Ohnosecond—That minuscule fraction of time in which you realize that you've just made a BIG mistake.

Percussive Maintenance—The fine art of whacking the daylights out of an electronic device to get it to work again.

Prairie Dogging—When someone yells or drops something loudly in a "cube farm" (an office full of cubicles) and all the co-workers' heads pop up over the walls to see what's going on.

Umfriend—A relationship of dubious standing or a concealed intimate relationship. (E.g., "This is Dale, my . . . um . . . friend.")

BLOOPER

Adult Sunday school mixer: Spelling be scheduled for Friday night.

QUOTE

How glorious a greeting the sun gives the mountains.—*John Muir*

·DAY·
175

Three elderly ladies were discussing the travails of getting older. One said, "Sometimes I catch myself in front of the refrigerator with a jar of mayonnaise in my hand, and I can't remember whether I need to put the jar away or start making a sandwich."

The second lady chimed in, "Yes, sometimes I find myself on the landing of the stairs and can't remember whether I was on my way up or down."

"Well, I'm glad I don't have that problem—knock on wood," the third one said as she rapped her knuckles on the table. "Oh! That must be the door—I'll get it!"

BLOOPER

Fourth and fifth graders' summer activities: Have fun around our campfire. Due to the ban on open fires, there will not be a fire.

QUOTE

In a gentle way, you can shake the world.—*Gandhi*

DAY 176

Insightful insights:

Time to lie on the beach. Yeah, I never tell the truth anywhere.

When repairmen say they'll "come sometime next week," I usually say, "Fine, I'll pay you sometime next year."

I'm a pretty patient person. Just as long as I'm not kept waiting for anything.

I use my cookbook often—to throw at people who suggest I cook.

I learned something important about burning leaves. Wait until they fall off the trees.

I'm thinking of renewing my vows . . . to never get married again.

Breaking up is hard to do. Unless you're mad and there's a vase nearby.

The best thing about late November is watching people who do homemade Christmas gifts start to really panic.

I enjoy battling mall crowds for the hot new Christmas toys. Oh, I don't buy the toy—I just like battling.

My personal goal for this year is to get in the way of other people's goals.

I cut my heating costs by 30 percent. Just let my legs go numb below the knee.

January is designated National Diet Month—mainly because December is National Eat-Like-a-Pig Month.

Thought about taking up snowboarding, but then I figured, why not just ram myself into a tree and save that long trip to the mountains.

The handy thing about credit cards is that they're a great way to pay off your credit cards.

BLOOPER

Ridge Street Lutheran: Quality, not quality, is our focus.

QUOTE

It is by acts and not ideas that people live.—*Harry Emerson Fosdick*

DAY 177

A burglar broke into a house one night. He shone his flashlight around, looking for valuables, and when he picked up a CD player to place in his sack, a strange, disembodied voice echoed in the dark: "Jesus is watching you."

He nearly jumped out of his skin, clicked his flashlight off, and froze. When he heard nothing more after a bit, he shook his head, promised himself a vacation after the next big score, then clicked the light back on and began searching for more valuables. Just as he pulled the stereo out so he could disconnect the wires, as clear as a bell he heard, "Jesus is watching you." Totally rattled, he shone his light around frantically, looking for the source of the voice. Finally, in the corner of the room, his flashlight beam came to rest on a parrot.

"Did you say that?" he hissed at the parrot.

"Yes," the parrot confessed, then squawked, "I'm just trying to warn you." The burglar relaxed. "Warn me, huh? Who do you think you are, anyway?"

"Moses," the bird replied.

"Moses!" The burglar laughed. "What kind of stupid people would name a parrot Moses?"

The bird answered, "The same kind of people who would name a Rottweiler Jesus!"

BLOOPER

Lake View Christian Elementary School: Excrelling in education for three decades.

QUOTE

Noble deeds that are concealed are most esteemed.—*Blaise Pascal*

·DAY·
178

A man finished reading the book *Man of the House* while riding the commuter train home from work. When he reached home, he stormed into the house and walked directly up to his wife. Pointing his finger in her face, he said, "From now on I want you to know that I am the man of this house, and my word is law! You are to prepare me a gourmet meal tonight, and when I'm finished eating my meal, I expect a sumptuous dessert afterward. Then, after dinner, you're going to draw my bath so I can relax. And when I'm finished with my bath, guess who's going to dress me and comb my hair?"

His wife thought for a moment and responded, "The funeral director is my guess."

BLOOPER

American Legion grapefruit will be available at the church through Sunday. Buy now before price is reduced.

QUOTE

There is nothing stronger in the world than gentleness.

179

A Sunday school teacher asked her class, "What was Jesus's mother's name?"

"Mary," one child answered.

The teacher then asked, "Who knows what Jesus's father's name was?"

"Verge," another kid said.

Confused, the teacher asked, "Where did you get that?"

The kid said, "Well, you know, they're always talking about Verge 'n' Mary."

BLOOPER	QUOTE
A seven-pound baby boy arrived last Tuesday to frighten the lives of Betty and John Forrest.	We are always on the anvil; by trials God is shaping us for higher things. —*Henry Ward Beecher*

180

Our first three babies, all girls, each weighed about seven pounds at birth. When our fourth arrived, he was much larger.

After delivery, the medical team began testing and measuring my new son. The last reading came from a nurse, who seemed impressed as she read, "Weight, nine pounds, eight ounces."

My husband, a CPA in corporate finance who'd been quiet up to this point, could contain himself no longer.

"How about that!" he exclaimed. "It's 36.5 percent more baby!"

BLOOPER	QUOTE
Pastor Denny and the youth group stopped at Carl's Bad Caverns on the way home from their mission trip.	A child of five would understand this. Send someone to fetch a child of five.—*Groucho Marx*

181

A man was driving down the highway late one night when his minivan broke down. He turned on his flashers and tried to get someone's attention to help him. Eventually a Lamborghini Countach pulled up.

"Any chance I could get a lift into town?" the minivan driver asked.

"I can do better than that," the man driving the Lamborghini replied. "I've got a V12 under this hood. I'm rich and can do what I want, so I had a tow hitch put on the car. I can tow you to the nearest town, no problem. Just honk your horn and flash your lights if I start going too fast."

They headed off down the road and eventually came to a stoplight, and up pulled a Ferrari Testarossa. The Ferrari began to rev its engine to get the Lamborghini to race. The Lamborghini revved its engine back, and the light turned green. They raced away from the stoplight, and about a half a mile down the road they passed a speed trap. By this time, they were simply flying.

The officer there watched them pass and radioed to base, saying, "Base, you will not believe what I just saw. A Ferrari and a Lamborghini were speeding down the road doing about 120, with a minivan honking its horn and flashing its lights trying to pass them!"

BLOOPER

Adult potluck: The church will be serving chicken wigs. Bring salad and drinks.

QUOTE

A friend doesn't go on a diet because you are fat.—*Erma Bombeck*

· DAY ·
182

The scene: Alexander Graham Bell's laboratory

An exciting new discovery is about to take place. Mr. Bell and his assistant, a man named Watson, have been hard at work on Bell's new invention to transmit sound over wires.

As Mr. Watson toils away in the room with the receiver, he suddenly hears *ring, ring, ring,* then . . .

"Good evening, sir. Are you paying too much for your long-distance service?"

BLOOPER

The Women's Guild of Neenah Baptist supports a woman's right to beast-feed in public.

QUOTE

A government that robs Peter to pay Paul can always depend on the support of Paul.—*George Bernard Shaw*

·DAY·

183

I was listening to a lady who called a radio pastor. The pastor was a wise, grandfatherly gentleman who had that calm, reassuring voice that can melt all fear. The lady, who was obviously crying, said, "Pastor, I've been blind all my life. I don't mind being blind, but I have some well-meaning friends who tell me that if I had more faith I could be healed."

The pastor asked her, "Tell me, do you carry one of those white canes?"

"Yes, I do," she replied.

"The next time someone says that, hit them over the head with the cane," he said. "Then tell them, 'If you had more faith, that wouldn't hurt!'"

BLOOPER	QUOTE
Patsy McCord of McCord's Diner has offered a special to all church members: buy one entrée and get something free.	A nickel ain't worth a dime anymore.—*Yogi Berra*

·DAY·

184

Arriving home from work at my usual hour of five p.m., I discovered that it had not been one of my wife's better days. Nothing I said or did seemed to be right.

By seven p.m., things had not changed, so I suggested I go outside, pretend I had just gotten home, and start all over again. My wife agreed.

I went outside, came back in, and announced with a big smile, "Honey, I'm home!"

"And just where have you been?" she replied sharply. "It's after seven o'clock!"

BLOOPER	QUOTE
Education expert Bert Fassets is offering a video to all parents. "It gets kids away from television," he said.	A word to the wise isn't necessary. It's the stupid people who need the advice.—*Bill Cosby*

A couple goes for a meal at a Chinese restaurant and orders the chicken surprise. The waiter brings the meal, served in a lidded, cast-iron pot.

Just as the wife is about to serve herself, the lid of the pot rises slightly, and she briefly sees two beady little eyes looking around before the lid slams back down.

"Good grief, did you see that?" she asks her husband.

He didn't, so she asks him to look in the pot. He reaches for it and again the lid rises, and he sees two little eyes looking around before it slams down.

Sputtering in a fit of pique, he calls the waiter over, describes what is happening, and demands an explanation.

"Please, sir," the waiter says, "what you order?"

The husband replies, "Chicken surprise."

"Ah, so sorry," the waiter says, "I bring you peeking duck."

BLOOPER

The office has issued the wrong dates for summer vacation Bible school. The bulletin stated it was July 5 to 9. It should have read July 5 to 9.

QUOTE

Alimony is like buying hay for a dead horse.—*Groucho Marx*

The restaurant where I took my two sons for a meal was crowded with fans watching a sporting event on television. The harried waitress took our order, but more than half an hour passed with no sign of her return.

I was trying to keep my kids from becoming restless when suddenly shouts of victory came from the bar.

"Hey," my eleven-year-old said, "it sounds as if someone just got his food."

BLOOPER

St. Albans Church family reunion to behead on Sunday, August 5.

QUOTE

Alright—everyone line up alphabetically by height.—*Casey Stengel*

·DAY·
187

When the office printer's type began to get garbled and faint, the office manager called a local repair shop, where a friendly man informed him that the printer probably needed only to be cleaned. Because the store charged fifty dollars for such cleanings, he said, the manager might try reading the printer's manual and doing the job himself.

Pleasantly surprised by his candor, the office manager asked, "Does your boss know that you discourage business?"

"Actually, it's my boss's idea," the employee replied. "We usually make more money on repairs if we let people try to fix things themselves first."

BLOOPER

The Ladies' Auxiliary will sponsor an "Enchanted South Pacific evening," complete with soothing Caribbean sounds from the Pleasant Hill High School steel drum band.

QUOTE

Cross-country skiing is great if you live in a small country.—*Steven Wright*

·DAY·
188

After watching the movie *Cinderella*, five-year-old Sarah started using her pinwheel as a magic wand, pretending she was a fairy godmother. "Make three wishes," she told her mother, "and I'll grant them."

Her mom first asked for world peace. Sarah swung her wand and proclaimed the request fulfilled.

Next, her mother requested a cure for all ill children. Again, with a sweep of the pinwheel, Sarah obliged.

The mother, with a glance down at her rather ample curves, made her third wish: "I wish to have a trim figure again."

The miniature fairy godmother started waving her wand madly and exclaimed, "I'll need more power for this!"

BLOOPER

Church bulletin board—For sale: Knock-Knacks—all sorts of collectibles and decorative items.

QUOTE

Electricity is really just organized lightning.

"Where is my Sunday paper?" the irate customer calling the newspaper office demanded.

"Ma'am," the newspaper employee said, "today is Saturday. The Sunday paper is not delivered until tomorrow, on Sunday."

There was quite a long pause on the other end of the phone, followed by a ray of recognition as she muttered, "Well, that explains why no one was at church today!"

BLOOPER

Regional church board assures deacons that ethics ordinance won't apply to elected officials.

QUOTE

Everyone knows how to raise children, except the people who have them.
—P. J. O'Rourke

A student came running in tears to her father. "Dad, you gave me some terrible financial advice!" she cried.

"I did? What did I tell you?" her dad asked.

"You told me to put my money in that big bank, and now that bank is in trouble."

"What are you talking about? That's one of the largest banks in the world," he said. "Surely there must be some mistake."

"I don't think so," she said. "They just returned one of my checks with a note saying 'insufficient funds.'"

BLOOPER

Church bulletin board: Pony for sale—looks like a small horse.

QUOTE

Everything is in walking distance if you have the time.

· DAY ·
191

Mr. Swiller was known far and wide as a hard-nosed boss who watched his employees like a hawk. He was making one of his regular tours of the factory when he spotted a young man leaning against a pile of boxes just outside the foreman's office. Since George, the foreman, wasn't around, Swiller watched to see just how long the young man would stand around doing nothing.

The young man yawned, scratched his head, looked at his watch, and sat on the floor, then leaned back on the pile of boxes.

Swiller stepped from his hiding place and walked up to the young man. "You!" he boomed. "How much do you make a week?"

The young man looked up. "Two hundred and fifty dollars," he said.

Swiller swooped into the cashier's office, took $250 from the cash box, and returned. "Take it," he said, "and get out! Don't let me see you around here again!"

The young man took the cash, put it in his pocket, and left.

Swiller snorted at his lack of remorse, embarrassment, or any other feeling. Then he went looking for George. When he found him, Swiller was red with anger. "That idler in front of your office," Swiller said. "I just gave him a week's pay and fired him. What's the matter with you, letting him stand around as though he had nothing to do?"

"You mean the kid in the red shirt?" George asked.

"Yes! The kid in the red shirt!"

"He was waiting for the twenty dollars we owe him for lunch," George said. "He works for the coffee shop around the corner."

BLOOPER	QUOTE
Gorillas of Rwanda lecture at summer seminar series at Kenilworth Evangelical.	Fashions have done more harm than revolutions.—*Victor Hugo*

A woman goes to the doctor for her yearly physical. The nurse starts with certain basic items. "How much do you weigh?" she asks.

"I weigh 120," the woman says. The nurse puts her on the scale. It turns out her weight is 150.

The nurse asks, "Your height?"

"Five feet, eight inches," she says. The nurse checks and sees that she measures only five feet, five inches.

The nurse takes the woman's blood pressure and tells her it's very high.

"Of course it's high!" she screams. "When I came in here, I was tall and slender, and now I'm short and fat!"

BLOOPER

Our outgoing pastor Greg Sallons wishes to thank the staff for their hard work and medication.

QUOTE

Food is a very important part of a balanced diet.

A boy was waiting on his mother to come out of a store. As he waited, he was approached by a man who asked, "Son, can you tell me where the post office is?"

The boy replied, "Sure, just go straight down the street a couple of blocks and turn to your right."

The man thanked the boy kindly and said, "I'm the new pastor at the Baptist church in town, and I'd like for you to come to church on Sunday. I'll show you how to get to heaven."

"Yeah, right," the boy replied with a chuckle. "You don't even know the way to the post office!"

BLOOPER

Church bulletin board—For sale: White trash compactor—new.

QUOTE

Get your facts first, then you can distort them later.—*Mark Twain*

DAY

194

Fresh out of business school, the young man answered a want ad for an accountant. He was being interviewed by a very nervous man who ran a three-man business.

"I need someone with an accounting degree," the man said. "But mainly I'm looking for someone to do my worrying for me."

"Excuse me?" the young accountant said.

"I worry about a lot of things," the man said. "But I don't want to have to worry about money. Your job will be to take all the money worries off my back."

"I see," the young accountant said. "And how much does the job pay?"

"I will start you at $85,000."

"Wow, $85,000!" the young man exclaimed. "How can such a small business afford a sum like that?"

"That," the man said, "is your first worry."

BLOOPER

Church bulletin board—For sale: 1997 Mercury Mistake.

QUOTE

Happiness is having a large, loving, caring, close-knit family in another city.—*George Burns*

DAY

195

My sister went to the department store to check out the bridal registry of our niece whose wedding was coming up soon. When she returned from the store, she tossed the gift list on a table and declared, "I think she's too young to get married."

"Why do you say that?" I asked.

"Because," she said, "they registered for video games."

BLOOPER

Regional Board of Deacons report calls on denomination headquarters to stop issuing so many denominational reports.

QUOTE

Human beings are the only creatures on earth who allow their children to come back home.—*Bill Cosby*

DAY 196

A couple of old guys were golfing when one said he was going to Dr. Taylor for a new set of dentures in the morning. His friend remarked that he had gone to the same dentist a few years before.

"Is that so?" the first said. "Did he do a good job?"

"Well, I was on the course yesterday when the fellow on the ninth hole hooked a shot," he said. "The ball must have been going two hundred miles per hour when it hit me in the stomach. That was the first time in two years my teeth didn't hurt."

BLOOPER

You'll like our church! We are located in a small, congenital neighborhood.

QUOTE

I always wanted to be somebody, but now I realize that I should have been more specific.—*Lily Tomlin*

DAY 197

God is sitting in heaven when a scientist says to him, "Lord, we don't need you anymore. Science has finally figured out a way to create life out of nothing. In other words, we can now do what you did in the beginning."

"Oh, is that so? Tell me," God says.

"Well," the scientist says, "we can take dirt and form it into your likeness and breathe life into it, thus creating man. Of course, we use sophisticated chemicals and lasers and lots of electricity. But it is life."

"Well, that's interesting. Show me."

The scientist bends down to the earth and starts to mold the soil.

"Oh, no, no, no," God interrupts. "Get your own dirt."

BLOOPER

While at the picnic this Sunday afternoon, remember to protect yourself from summer fun.

QUOTE

I buy expensive suits. They just look cheap on me.—*Warren Buffet*

198

There was a knock at my door. It was a small boy, about six years old. Something of his had found its way into my garage, he said, and he wanted it back.

Upon opening the garage door, I noticed two additions: a baseball and a broken window sporting a baseball-sized hole. "How do you suppose this ball got in here?" I asked the boy.

Taking one look at the ball, one look at the window, and one look at me, the boy exclaimed, "Wow! I must have thrown it right through that hole!"

 BLOOPER

The elders said the election will be held on January 22 or February 5, whichever comes first.

 QUOTE

The trouble is, if you don't risk anything, you risk even more.

199

More modern laws:

When you wish to unlock a door but have only one hand free, the keys are in the opposite pocket. (Von Fumbles Law)

A door will swing shut only when you have left the keys inside. (Yale Law of Destiny)

When your hands are covered with oil, grease, or glue, your nose will start to itch. (Law of Ichiban)

Your insurance will cover everything but what has happened. (Insurance So Sorry Law)

When things seem to be going well, you've probably forgotten to do something. (Cheney's Second Corollary)

When things seem easy to do, it's because you haven't followed all the instructions. (Destiny Awaits Law)

If you keep your cool when everyone else is losing theirs, it's probably because you have not realized the seriousness of the problem. (Law of Gravitas)

Most problems are not created or solved; they only change appearances. (Einstein's Law of Persistence)

BLOOPER

Church bulletin board: Free to good home—cat, neutered and sprayed.

QUOTE

I don't think anyone should write their autobiography until after they're dead.—*Samuel Goldwyn*

·DAY· 200

Little Susie, a six-year-old, came home from school and said, "Mommy, I've got a stomachache."

"That's because your stomach is empty," her mother replied. "You'd feel better if you had something in it." She gave Susie a snack, and sure enough, Susie felt better right away.

That afternoon the family's minister dropped by. While he was chatting with Susie's mom, he mentioned he'd had a bad headache all day long.

Susie perked up. "That's because it's empty," she said. "You'd feel better if you had something in it."

BLOOPER

Elders board: Treasurer arrested with church funds said, "I'm guilty, but not that guilty."

QUOTE

The human brain starts working the moment you are born and never stops until you stand up to speak in public.

·DAY· 201

Little Johnny asked his grandma how old she was. Grandma answered, "Thirty-nine and holding."

Johnny thought for a moment and then said, "And how old would you be if you let go?"

BLOOPER

The break-in at the parsonage occurred between November and Thursday.

QUOTE

I have never been hurt by what I have not said.—*Calvin Coolidge*

· DAY ·
202

A little boy in church for the first time watched as the ushers passed around the offering plates. When they came near his pew, the boy said loudly, "Don't pay for me, Daddy. I'm under five."

BLOOPER

Elder Dave will pass his gravel this Sunday during the business meeting.

QUOTE

I like long walks—especially when they are taken by people who annoy me.—*Fred Allen*

· DAY ·
203

I wanted to buy a CD player but was completely perplexed by one model's promotional sign. I called the sales clerk over and asked, "What does 'hybrid pulse D/A converter' mean?"

He said, "That means that this machine will read the digital information encoded on CDs and convert it into an audio signal."

"In other words," I said, "this CD player plays CDs."

"Exactly."

BLOOPER

On President's Day, the church Sunday school classes will celebrate Benjamin Franklin.

QUOTE

I never said most of the things I said.—*Yogi Berra*

· DAY ·
204

The preacher was having a heart-to-heart talk with a backslider of his flock, whose drinking of moonshine invariably led to quarreling with his neighbors and occasional shotgun blasts at some of them.

"Can't you see," the parson said, "that not one good thing comes out of this drinking?"

"Well, I sort of disagree there," the backslider replied. "It makes me miss the folks when I shoot at them."

BLOOPER

There is a 10:30 a.m. worship service and candle lighting in remembrance of all those who have died in the previous year at both services.

QUOTE

I sang in the church choir for years, even though my family belonged to another church.—*Paul Lynde*

A blonde policewoman pulls over a blonde girl in a convertible sports car for speeding. She walks up to the car and asks the blonde for her driver's license. The driver searches through her purse in vain. Finally, she asks, "What does it look like?"

The police officer tells her, "It's that thing with your picture on it." The driver searches for a few more seconds, pulls out her compact, opens it, and sees herself.

She hands the compact to the cop. After a few seconds looking at the compact, the blonde cop rolls her eyes, hands the compact back to the blonde convertible driver, and says, "If you would have told me you were a police officer when I first pulled you over, we could have avoided this whole thing."

BLOOPER

Denominational report: Average pastor is 44 years old and 31 percent female.

QUOTE

I got married by a judge. I should have asked for a jury.—*Groucho Marx*

DAY 206

A guy was watching TV as his wife was out cutting the grass during the hot summer. He finally worked up the energy to go out and ask his wife what was for supper.

Well, his missus was quite irritated about him sitting in the air-conditioned house while she did all the work. "I can't believe you're asking me about supper right now! Imagine I'm out of town. Go inside and figure out dinner yourself."

So he went back into the house and fixed himself a big steak with potatoes, garlic bread, and a tall glass of iced tea.

The wife finally walked in about the time he was finishing and asked him, "You fixed something to eat? So where's mine?"

He said, "Huh? I thought you were out of town."

BLOOPER

Seniors' Night Out will feature excellently repaired food.

QUOTE

I'm an idealist. I don't know where I'm going, but I'm on my way.—*Carl Sandburg*

DAY 207

Needing to shed a few pounds, my wife and I went on a diet that had specific recipes for each meal of the day. We followed the instructions closely, dividing the finished recipe in half for our individual plates. We felt terrific and thought the diet was wonderful—we never even felt hungry!

But soon we realized we were gaining weight, not losing it. Checking the recipes again, we found it. There, in fine print, was: "Serves 6."

BLOOPER

Following the silent auction, there will be a seven-corpse dinner.

QUOTE

If truth is beauty, how come no one has their hair done in the library?—*Lily Tomlin*

John, a neighbor, told me how his hearing aid occasionally emits a high-pitched squeal that can be heard by anyone near him. His granddaughter was sitting on his lap one day when the device started to beep.

Surprised, little Lorraine looked up at him and said, "Oh, Grampa, you've got email!"

BLOOPER

Sermon title: "As Winter Turns to Fall."

QUOTE

My computer beat me at chess, but I sure beat it at kickboxing.—*Emo Phillips*

A farmer gets sent to jail over a minor offense, and his wife is trying to hold the farm together until her husband can get out. She's not, however, very good at farm work, so she writes to him in jail: "Dear sweetheart, I want to plant the potatoes. When is the best time to do it?"

The farmer writes back: "Honey, don't go near that field. That's where all my guns are buried."

But because he is in jail, all of the farmer's mail is censored. So when the sheriff and his deputies read his letter, they all run out to the farm and dig up the entire potato field looking for guns. After two full days of digging, they don't find one single weapon.

The farmer then writes to his wife: "Honey, now is when you should plant the potatoes."

BLOOPER

Sermon title: "Time Is My Enema."

QUOTE

My theory is that all of Scottish cuisine is based on a dare.—*Mike Myers*

DAY
210

As heard at the information kiosks manned by Parks Canada staff:

How do the elk know they're supposed to cross at the "Elk Crossing" signs?

At what elevation does an elk become a moose?

Are the bears with collars tame?

Is there anywhere I can see the bears pose?

Is it okay to keep bacon on the picnic table, or should I store it in my tent?

I saw an animal on the way to Banff today—could you tell me what it was?

Did I miss the turnoff for Canada?

Where does Alberta end and Canada begin?

Do you have a map of the state of Jasper?

Is this the part of Canada that speaks French, or is that Saskatchewan?

What's the best way to see Canada in a day?

Where can I buy a raccoon hat? All Canadians own one, don't they?

Are there phones in Banff?

So it's eight kilometers away . . . is that in miles?

We're on the decibel system, you know.

Is that two kilometers by foot or by car?

BLOOPER

If any members have an extra pick nick table, please bring it to the church on Saturday.

QUOTE

Never have more children than you have car windows.—*Erma Bombeck*

DAY
211

Punnies:

"I can't believe I ate that whole pineapple!" Bill said dolefully.

"I haven't caught a fish all day!" Mike said without debate.

"I won't let a stupid flat tire let me down," Steve said with despair.

"I keep banging my head on things," Marty said bashfully.

"That is the second time my teacher changed my grade," Donna remarked.

"The fur is falling out of that mink coat," Steven inferred.

"That's the second electric shock that I've gotten today!" Stew said, revolted.

"I'll just have to send that telegram again," Samuel said remorsefully.

"I've been sick and lost a lot of weight," Rachel expounded.

BLOOPER

Property committee chairman Dick Farber said that the new facility will include fire-retardant toilet seats.

QUOTE

Older people should not eat health food. They need all the preservatives they can get.

·DAY·
212

During a summer break from my studies at an engineering university, I worked in a scrap yard repairing construction equipment. One afternoon I was taking apart a piling hammer that had some very large bolts holding it together. One of the nuts had corroded onto the bolt, so I started heating the nut with an oxyacetylene torch. As I was doing this, one of the dimmest apprentices I have ever known came along and asked me what I was doing. I patiently explained that if I heated the nut, it would grow larger and release its grip on the bolt so I could then remove it.

"So things get larger when they get hot, do they?" he asked.

Suddenly, an idea flashed into my mind. "Yes," I said, "that's why days are longer in summer and shorter in winter."

There was a long pause, then his face cleared. "You know, I always wondered about that," he said.

BLOOPER

Pastor's folly: "God is always searching our hearts and minds—just like Santa Claus."

QUOTE

Originality is the art of remembering what you hear but forgetting where you heard it.—*Laurence J. Peter*

DAY 213

I was having trouble with my computer, so I called Harold, the computer guy, to come over. Harold clicked a couple of buttons and solved the problem. He gave me a bill for a minimum service call.

As he was walking away, I called after him, "So, what was wrong?"

"It was an ID Ten T error," he replied.

I didn't want to appear stupid, but I nonetheless asked, "An ID Ten T error? What's that, in case I need to fix it again?"

Harold grinned. "Haven't you ever heard of an ID Ten T error before?"

"No," I replied.

"Write it down," he said, "and I think you'll figure it out."

So I wrote it down.

I D 1 0 T

I used to like Harold . . .

BLOOPER

Pastor Good asked the church body for patients.

QUOTE

Parents are the last people on earth who should have children.

DAY 214

In a rush to work one morning, I pulled up to the drive-through window at a fast-food restaurant and ordered some coffee.

Because I was in a hurry, I asked them to put a couple of ice cubes in the coffee so it would cool down quicker and I could drink it faster.

I sat there at the pick-up window for a few minutes, wondering where they had to go to get my coffee, when a frustrated teenager finally came up and said, "I'm sorry for the delay, but the ice you wanted in your coffee keeps melting!"

BLOOPER

Sermon title: "Quality You Can't Count On."

QUOTE

Procrastination is the art of keeping up with yesterday.

· DAY ·
215

A couple months ago, I entered a contest and ended up winning a few acres of swampland below the floodplain in Mississippi. Before I knew it, I won a $250,000 house, so naturally I built it on my new land. Last week, I won enough money in the lottery to quit my job and move down there for good. And just last night, as I sat on my new porch watching the rain and listening to the thunder, it all started to sink in.

BLOOPER

Betty Amber, the director of the church preschool program, reminded parents that she is "not happy until they're not happy."

QUOTE

Recession is when your neighbor loses his job. Depression is when you lose yours.—*Ronald Reagan*

· DAY ·
216

A naive young girl was playing Trivial Pursuit one night. It was her turn. She rolled the dice and landed on Science & Nature.

Her question was, "If you are in a vacuum and someone calls your name, can you hear it?"

She thought for a minute or two and then asked, "Is it on or off?"

BLOOPER

The missions conference will feature food from the Orient, including chimp chow mein.

QUOTE

Start each day with a smile and get it over with.—*W. C. Fields*

· DAY ·
217

The policeman couldn't believe his eyes when he saw a woman drive past him on the freeway, busily knitting. Quickly he pulled alongside the vehicle, rolled down his window, and shouted, "Pull over!"

"No," the women called back cheerfully. "Socks!"

BLOOPER

The 25rd annual all-church picnic will be held this Saturday.

QUOTE

Television is a medium because anything well done is rare.—*Fred Allen*

DAY 218

The day after a young couple had returned from their honeymoon, the bride called her mother in a panic.

"What's the matter, dear? Was the honeymoon dreadful?"

"No, but oh, Mama! As soon as we got home, he started using the most horrible language! Horrible four-letter words!"

"Darling, shh," her mother said. "Calm down and tell me what he said that was so awful."

"Oh, Mama, it's so embarrassing," the still-sobbing bride said. "He said words like *cook*, *iron*, *wash*, *dust*!"

BLOOPER

Sermon title: "Do You Get Your Advice by Reading 'Dead Abby'?"

QUOTE

The only time a woman really succeeds in changing a man is when he is a baby.

DAY 219

A sloth named Herman is walking through the forest one day. A gang of snails approaches him and beats him up. He is left at the bottom of a tree with several cuts and bruises.

Several hours later, he gathers up enough strength to go to a local police station and walks into the sergeant's office.

"What happened to you?" the officer asks.

"A gang of snails beat me up," Herman replies.

"Can you describe what they looked like?"

"I don't know," the sloth says. "It all happened so fast."

BLOOPER

Vermont Valley Bible Church will be selling their unused parsonage. This is a lovely home, featuring a ceiling in every room.

QUOTE

When I was a boy, the Dead Sea was only sick. —*George Burns*

King Ozymandias of Assyria was running low on cash after years of war with the Hittites. His last great possession was the Star of the Euphrates, the most valuable diamond in the ancient world. Desperate, he went to Croesus, the pawnbroker, to get a loan.

"I'll give you 100,000 dinars for it," Croesus said.

"But I paid a million dinars for it," the king protested. "Don't you know who I am? I am the king!"

Croesus replied, "When you wish to pawn a star, makes no difference who you are."

BLOOPER

Church bulletin board—For sale: Potty chair, oak, handmade, dark brown stain.

QUOTE

You are only as good as your last haircut.

Mrs. Golden was shopping at a produce stand in her neighborhood. She approached a vendor and asked, "How much are these oranges?"

"Two for a quarter," the vendor said.

"How much is just one?" she asked.

"Fifteen cents," the vendor answered.

"Then I'll take the other one."

BLOOPER

Due to the growing size of our nursery, we will be splitting infants and toddlers.

QUOTE

I broke up with my girlfriend, and she said I would never find anyone like her again. Well, I hope not. If I didn't want her, why would I want someone just like her?

• DAY •
222

One Sunday morning when my son was about five years old, we were attending church in our community. It was common for the preacher to invite the children to the front of the church and have a short lesson before beginning the sermon. He would bring in an item they could find around the house and relate it to a teaching from the Bible.

This particular morning, the visual aid for his lesson was a smoke detector. He asked the children if anyone knew what it meant when an alarm sounded from the smoke detector.

My child immediately raised his hand and said, "It means Daddy's cooking dinner."

BLOOPER

Please note: In correcting the incorrect statement, we published the incorrect correction.

QUOTE

Dogs have owners; cats have staff.

• DAY •
223

Ten ways the Bible would be different if written by college students:

10. The Last Supper would be eaten the next morning—cold.
9. The Ten Commandments would actually be only five, double-spaced, written in a large font.
8. There would be a new edition every two years in order to limit reselling.
7. Forbidden fruit would have been eaten because it wasn't cafeteria food.
6. Paul's letter to the Romans would become Paul's email to abuse@romans.gov.
5. The reason Cain killed Abel: they were roommates.
4. The place where the end of the world occurs: finals, not Armageddon.
3. Out would go the mules, in would come the mountain bikes.
2. The reason why Moses and followers walked in the desert for forty years: they didn't want to ask for directions and look like freshmen.
1. Instead of God creating the world in six days and resting on the seventh, he would have put off creation until the night before it was due and then pulled an all-nighter.

BLOOPER

As a fund-raising campaign, the young people of the church will be selling frozen hamburger patties from Al's Meats. The delicious patties are made with 85 percent fresh ground beef.

QUOTE

Everyone has a photographic memory. Some don't have film.

· DAY ·
224

A blonde, wanting to earn some extra money, decided to hire herself out as a handywoman and started canvassing the neighborhood. She went to the front door of the first house and asked the owner if he had any odd jobs for her to do.

"Well, I guess I could use somebody to paint my porch," he said. "How much will you charge me?"

The blonde quickly responded, "How about a hundred dollars?"

The man agreed and told her that the paint and everything she would need was in the garage.

A short time later, the blonde handywoman came to the door to collect her money.

"You can't be finished already," the man said.

"Yes, I am," the blonde replied, "and I had paint left over, so I gave it two coats—no extra charge."

Impressed, the man reached into his pocket for the hundred dollars and handed it to her.

"By the way," the blonde added, "it's not a Porch—it's a Lexus."

BLOOPER

Paul and Edna Dister are offering a reward. Following the funeral at church, they discovered that their parents' ashes, in urns, were taken from their garbage can.

QUOTE

Borrow money from a pessimist. They don't expect it back.

· DAY · 225

A young and foolish pilot wanted to sound cool on the aviation frequencies. On his first time approaching a field during the nighttime, instead of making any official request to the tower, he said, "Guess who?"

The controller switched the field lights off and replied, "Guess where!"

BLOOPER

The church will be passing out red roses this Sunday to all mothers. Give this rose to your mom—or someone you really care about.

QUOTE

Someone complimented me on my driving today. They left a little note on the windshield that said "Parking Fine."

· DAY · 226

Insightful insights:

I used to live in a house by the freeway. When I went anywhere, I had to be going sixty-five miles per hour by the end of my driveway.

I was once walking through the forest alone. A tree fell right in front of me—and I didn't hear it.

I watched the Indy 500, and I was thinking that if they left earlier, they wouldn't have to go so fast.

I went to a restaurant that serves "breakfast at any time." So I ordered French toast during the Renaissance.

I've got some powdered water, but I don't know what to add.

I'm writing a book. I've got the page numbers done.

If toast always lands butter-side down, and cats always land on their feet, what happens if you strap toast on the back of a cat and drop it?

It doesn't make a difference what temperature a room is, it's always room temperature.

It's a small world, but I wouldn't want to paint it.

My friend Winnie is a procrastinator. He didn't get his birthmark until he was eight years old.

My friend has a baby. I'm writing down all the noises the baby makes so later I can ask him what he meant.

BLOOPER

Silent auction item: Man's Swiss-made wristwatch—works made in Japan, assembled in Italy.

QUOTE

Just because no one complains, it doesn't mean that all parachutes are perfect.

A Sunday school teacher decided to have her young class memorize one of the most-quoted passages in the Bible: Psalm 23. She gave the youngsters a month to learn the chapter.

Little Rick was excited about the task, but he just couldn't remember the Psalm. Even after much practice, he could barely get past the first line.

On the day that the kids were scheduled to recite Psalm 23 in front of the congregation, Rick was very nervous. When it was his turn, he stepped up to the microphone and said, "The Lord is my shepherd, and that's all I need to know."

BLOOPER

Church newsletter—For sale: Snowblower. Five horsepower. Worked great last summer.

QUOTE

Suppose you were an idiot and suppose you were a member of Congress. But I repeat myself.—*Mark Twain*

Late one night, a man walks into a dentist's surgery and says, "Excuse me, can you help me? I think I'm a moth."

"You don't need a dentist. You need a psychiatrist," the dentist says.

"Yes, I know," the man replies.

"So why did you come in here?" the dentist asks.

"Well, the light was on."

BLOOPER

Pastor's folly: Yom Kippur—Dave of Atonement.

QUOTE

Life begins at 40—but so do bad arches, arthritis, faulty eyesight, and the tendency to tell a story to the same person three or four times.—*Helen Rowland*

·DAY· 229

A young mother was riding the bus with her four-year-old boy when he suddenly blurted out so that everyone on the bus could hear: "Look, Mom, see that man's nose? It looks soooo funny!"

The mother was quite embarrassed and scolded her son. Then she whispered to him that if he wanted to say something about someone, he had to wait until they got home, or at least where nobody could hear them, so that nobody would be sad.

A moment later, the boy blurted out in the same loud voice: "Look, Mom, we've got to talk about that big fat lady when we get home!"

BLOOPER

School menu: Tuesday—kosher hot dogs wrapped in bacon.

QUOTE

An archaeologist is the best husband a woman could have. The older she gets, the more interested he is in her. —*Agatha Christie*

·DAY· 230

A clergyman walking down a country lane saw a young man struggling to load hay back onto a cart after it had fallen off.

"You look tired, my son," the cleric said. "Why don't you rest a moment and I'll give you a hand?"

"No thanks," the young man said. "My father wouldn't approve."

"Don't be silly," the minister said. "Everyone is entitled to a break. Come and have a drink of water."

Again the young man protested that his father would be upset.

Losing his patience just a little, the clergyman said, "Your father must be a real slave driver. Tell me where I can find him and I'll give him a piece of my mind!"

"Well," the young farmer replied, "you can tell him whatever you like just as soon as I get this hay off him."

BLOOPER

Rent-a-Teen Fund-Raiser: "We'll clean your house for you. Why risk a poor-quality cleaning job when we guarantee it?"

QUOTE

I hope that after I die people will say of me: "That guy sure owed me a lot of money."

An arrogant Department of Agriculture (DOA) representative stopped at a farm and told the old farmer, "I need to inspect your farm."

"Okay, but you better not go in that field," the old farmer said.

"I have the authority of the US government with me," the agricultural representative said. "See this card? I am allowed to go wherever I wish on agricultural land."

So the old farmer went about his farm chores. Later he heard loud screams. He saw the DOA rep running for the fence, and close behind was the farmer's prize bull. The bull was madder than a nest of hornets and was gaining at every step.

The old farmer called out, "Show him your card!"

BLOOPER

Men's Fraternity is looking for fathers. Attention, all dads between 12 and 25.

QUOTE

Quidquid latine dictum sit, altum videtur. (Anything said in Latin sounds profound.)

Retirement questions and answers:

Question: When is a retiree's bedtime?
Answer: Three hours after he falls asleep in his chair.

Question: Why don't retirees mind being called seniors?
Answer: The term comes with a 10 percent discount.

Question: Among retirees, what is considered formal attire?
Answer: Tied shoes.

Question: Why are retirees so slow to clean out the basement, attic, or garage?
Answer: They know that as soon as they do, one of their adult kids will want to store stuff there.

Question: What's the biggest advantage of going back to school as a retiree?
Answer: If you cut classes, no one calls your parents.

BLOOPER

Free to good home: Shemale German shepherd.

QUOTE

Analyzing humor is like dissecting a frog—only a few people are interested and the frog dies.—*E. B. White*

DAY 233

Computer truths:

As soon as you delete a worthless file, you'll need it.

Installing a new program will always mess up at least one old one.

You can't win them all, but you sure can lose them all.

The likelihood of a hard drive crash is in direct proportion to the value of the material that hasn't been backed up.

There are only two kinds of computer users: those whose hard drives have crashed, and those whose hard drives haven't crashed—yet.

Anything can be made to work if you fiddle with it. If you fiddle with something long enough, you'll break it.

BLOOPER

Herald City Baptist 10th Annual Fish Fry to feature chicken.

QUOTE

The tooth fairy encourages kids to sell body parts.

DAY 234

There's an old story about a mother who walks in on her six-year-old son and finds him sobbing. "What's the matter?" she asks.

"I've just figured out how to tie my shoes."

"Well, honey, that's wonderful." Being a wise mother, she recognizes his victory in the Eriksonian struggle of autonomy versus doubt. "You're growing up, but why are you crying?"

"Because," he says, "now I'll have to do it every day for the rest of my life."

BLOOPER

Sermon title: "The Safer You Are, the More You Are Safe."

QUOTE

A good lawyer knows the law; a clever lawyer takes the judge to lunch.

I have a friend who always seemed to lean slightly to the left all the time. It used to bother me, so I suggested he see a doctor and have his legs checked out.

For years, he refused and told me I was crazy. But last week, he finally went, and sure enough, the doctor discovered his left leg was a quarter inch shorter than his right.

A quick bit of orthopedic surgery later, he was cured. Both legs are exactly the same length now, and he no longer leans.

"So," I said, "you didn't believe me when I told you a doctor could fix your leg."

He looked at me and said, "I stand corrected."

BLOOPER

The Bogger Church youth car wash guarantees your 10 percent satisfaction with a job well done.

QUOTE

Life is pleasant. Death is peaceful. It's the transition between that is troublesome.—*Isaac Asimov*

My pastor friend put sanitary hot-air hand dryers in the restrooms at his church, but after two weeks he took them out.

I asked him why, and he confessed that they worked fine, but when he went into the men's restroom, he saw a sign that read:

"For a sample of this week's sermon, push the button."

BLOOPER

Pastor's folly: On a scale of 1 to 10, this is an A.

QUOTE

Trouble defies the law of gravity. It is easier to pick up than it is to drop.

· DAY ·
237

What is marketing?

You see a gorgeous girl at a party. You go up to her and say, "I am very rich. Marry me!" That's direct marketing.

You're at a party with a bunch of friends and see a gorgeous girl. One of your friends goes up to her, points at you, and says, "He's very rich. Marry him." That's advertising.

You see a gorgeous girl at a party. You go up to her and get her telephone number. The next day you call and say, "Hi, I'm very rich. Marry me." That's telemarketing.

You're at a party and see a gorgeous girl. You straighten your tie; you compliment her hair. You open the door for her, offer her a ride, and then say, "By the way, I'm very rich. Will you marry me?" That's public relations.

You're at a party and see a gorgeous girl. She walks up to you and says, "You are very rich . . ." That's brand recognition.

You see a gorgeous girl at a party. You go up to her and say, "I'm rich. Marry me." She gives you a nice hard slap on your face. That's customer feedback.

BLOOPER

Church asks for help: Police plan to keep an eye on nude beach activities.

QUOTE

Foolproof plans do not take into account the ingenuity of fools.

· DAY ·
238

A man was wheeling himself frantically down the hall of the hospital in his wheelchair just before his operation.

A nurse stopped him and asked, "What's the matter?"

He said, "I heard the nurse say, 'It's a very simple operation, so don't worry. I'm sure it will be all right.'"

"She was just trying to comfort you. What's so frightening about that?"

"She wasn't talking to me. She was talking to the doctor!"

BLOOPER

High school youth group member Randy Thermon competes in the 50-mile and 100-mile dash.

QUOTE

Income tax has made more liars out of the American people than golf.—*Will Rogers*

· DAY ·
239

My son, Ken, was married yesterday. I heard him tell his bride, Caryn, that his ring was so tight it was cutting off his circulation. She replied, "That's what it's supposed to do."

BLOOPER

Women's Guild of Fox Valley Christian Center will hold a whine and cheese party as their summer kickoff event.

QUOTE

Why does a slight tax increase cost you $200 and a substantial tax cut save you 30 cents?

· DAY ·
240

Wanda's dishwasher quit working, so she called a repairman. Since she had to go to work the next day, she told the repairman, "I'll leave the key under the mat. Fix the dishwasher, leave the bill on the counter, and I'll mail you a check. Oh, by the way, don't worry about my bulldog. He won't bother you. But whatever you do, do *not*, under *any* circumstances, talk to my parrot! I repeat, *do not* talk to my parrot!"

When the repairman arrived at Wanda's apartment the following day, he discovered the biggest, meanest-looking bulldog he had ever seen. But, just as she had said, the dog just lay there on the carpet, watching the repairman go about his work.

The parrot, however, drove him nuts the whole time with his incessant yelling and name calling. Finally, the repairman couldn't contain himself any longer and yelled, "Shut up, you stupid, ugly bird!"

To which the parrot replied, "Get him, Spike!"

BLOOPER

Church bulletin board—For sale: 4-year-old beagle mix. Runs good.

QUOTE

To stop smoking is the easiest thing. I should know—I've done it a thousand times.—*Mark Twain*

· DAY ·
241

Joey and his classmates had just finished a tour of the local fire hall. Before each student could leave, the fire chief quizzed them. He asked little Joey, "What do you do if your clothes catch on fire?"

Joey replied promptly, "I don't put them on."

BLOOPER

Bride Annette Benidt and Goom Randy Cummings will be united this Saturday.

QUOTE

One has fear in front of a goat, in back of a mule, and on every side of a fool.

· DAY ·
242

One Sunday morning, everyone in a bright, beautiful, tiny town got up early and went to the local church. Before the services started, the townspeople were sitting in their pews and talking about their lives, their families, and the like.

Suddenly, in a cloud of fire and brimstone, Satan appeared at the front of the church. Everyone started screaming and running for the front entrance, trampling each other in a frantic effort to get away from evil incarnate.

Soon everyone was evacuated from the church, except for one elderly gentleman who sat calmly in his pew, not moving, seemingly oblivious to the fact that God's ultimate enemy was in his presence. Satan was more than a little confused, so he walked up to the man and said, "Don't you know who I am?"

"Yep, sure do," the man replied.

"Aren't you afraid of me?" Satan asked.

"Nope, sure ain't," the man said.

Satan was a little perturbed at this and queried, "Why aren't you afraid of me?"

The man calmly replied, "Been married to your sister for over forty-eight years."

BLOOPER

Pastor's folly: Global worming a threat to all.

QUOTE

My formula for success is rise early, work late, and strike oil. —*J. Paul Getty*

Kid wisdom:

When your dad is mad and asks you, "Do I look stupid?" don't answer.

Never tell your mom her diet's not working.

Stay away from prunes.

Don't pull your dad's finger when he tells you to.

Never leave your three-year-old brother in the same room as your school assignment.

If you want a kitten, start out by asking for a horse.

Felt-tip markers are not good to use as lipstick.

Don't pick on your sister when she's holding a baseball bat.

When you get a bad grade in school, show it to your mom when she's on the phone.

BLOOPER

Geek Orthodox congregation of Lyons Township is planning to build a new church.

QUOTE

It's not my fault that I never learned to accept responsibility.

· DAY ·
244

You know how hard it is to talk to your dentist when your teeth are being cleaned or you're getting a filling? Well, I decided I would make up a sort of sign language that you could use to express yourself without having to mumble. These would be printed on a poster and mounted on the ceiling above the dentist chair.

This list would give you something to read since procedures can be boring. When a phrase seems appropriate, you would just hold up the corresponding number of fingers to express yourself. The dentist would not need to stop to ask you to repeat yourself and could fix the problem right away.

1. Everything is fine, but my nose itches.
2. There seems to be spit running down my neck.
3. So, I guess you had garlic for lunch today?
4. You realize that wasn't my tooth you just poked with that incredibly sharp tool of yours, right?
5. I would *really* prefer that you not do that again.
6. Could you please suction the chunk of debris that you missed before I gag?
7. Remember how I said I was numb? I think I may have been mistaken.
8. Wait a minute—maybe I am allergic to latex.
9. Just so you know, if I don't get to take a break soon, I may bite you.
10. Please stop asking me stupid questions about myself, or I will take that paper mask off your face.

BLOOPER

Church bulletin board—For sale: American flag—sixty-star model, with pole.

QUOTE

Marriage is when a man and a woman become one. The trouble starts when they try to decide which one.

· DAY ·
245

A tourist is traveling with a guide through one of the thickest jungles in Latin America when he comes across an ancient Mayan temple. The tourist is entranced by the temple and asks the guide for details. The guide states that archaeologists are carrying out excavations and are still finding great treasures. The tourist then asks how old the temple is.

"This temple is 2,503 years old," the guide says.

Impressed at this accurate dating, the tourist asks how he knew this precise figure.

"Easy," the guide replies. "The archaeologists said the temple was 2,500 years old, and that was three years ago."

BLOOPER

Please note: Cans of cat and dog are appreciated at DuPage Church food pantry.

QUOTE

Never wear a backward baseball cap to a job interview unless you're applying for the job of an umpire.

·DAY·
246

Redneck movie quotes:

"We'll always have Walmart."

"You had me at 'Sooooey!'"

"Houston, we have a possum."

"Are you *crying*? There's no crying in NASCAR!"

"Of all the trailer parks in Pine Cone County, she had to pull her '68 Rambler into mine."

"Use the horse, Luke!"

"Hokey opera and ancient museums are no match for a good tractor pull, kid."

"I know what you're thinking: did he fire six shots or only five? Well, heck if I know! You *know* I can't count no higher'n three since the chainsaw accident!"

"You want a tooth? You can't *handle* a tooth!"

BLOOPER

Congratulations! Church member Jim Moore received the first annual Jim Moore award in a ceremony last week.

QUOTE

The trouble with being punctual is that there is no one there to appreciate it.

247

Punny truisms:

When a clock is hungry, it goes back four seconds.

The guy who fell onto an upholstery machine was fully recovered.

A grenade fell onto a kitchen floor in France, resulting in Linoleum Blownapart.

You are stuck with your debt if you can't budge it.

He broke into song because he couldn't find the key.

A calendar's days are numbered.

A lot of money is tainted: 'taint yours and 'taint mine.

A boiled egg is hard to beat.

He had a photographic memory that was never developed.

A plateau is a high form of flattery.

Those who get too big for their britches will be exposed in the end.

When you've seen one shopping center, you've seen a mall.

When she saw her first strands of gray hair, she thought she'd dye.

Bakers trade bread recipes on a knead-to-know basis.

Santa's helpers are subordinate clauses.

Acupuncture is a jab well done.

BLOOPER

Getting married? Planning a wedding? At Highland Park Bible Church, we provide a hospital room for the bridal party.

QUOTE

Advice is what we ask for when we already know the answer but wish we didn't.

248

Passengers aboard a luxurious cruise ship were having a great time when a beautiful young woman fell overboard. Immediately there was an eighty-year-old man in the water who rescued her.

The crew pulled them both out of the treacherous waters. The captain was grateful as well as astonished that the white-haired old man performed such an act of bravery. That night a banquet was given in honor of the ship's elderly hero. He was called forward to receive an award and was asked to say a few words.

He said, "First of all, I'd like to know who pushed me."

BLOOPER

Ginger West is recovering at home, having had an operation for her carpet tunnel syndrome.

QUOTE

Money will not buy happiness, but it will pay the salaries of a large research staff to study the problem.

DAY 249

Miss Jones had been giving her second-grade students a lesson on science. She had explained about magnets and showed how they would pick up nails and other bits of iron. Now it was question time, so she asked, "My name begins with the letter 'M,' and I pick up things. What am I?"

A little boy in the front row said, "You're a mother."

BLOOPER

Men's breakfast at St. Michael's will include Spam, which is now in season.

QUOTE

Beware of the young doctor and the old barber.—*Benjamin Franklin*

DAY 250

At the end of the college year, a star football player celebrated the relaxation of team curfew by attending a late-night campus party. Soon after arriving, he became captivated by a beautiful young woman and eased into a conversation with her by asking if she met many dates at parties.

"Oh, I have a 3.9, so I'm much more attracted to the strong academic types than to dumb party animals," she said. "What's your GPA?"

Grinning from ear to ear, the jock boasted, "I get about 27 in the city and 38 on the highway."

BLOOPER

The church office will be closed July 4 in observance of Memorial Day.

QUOTE

If you die in an elevator, make sure you press the up button.—*Sam Levenson*

251 Rules for city driving:

Never, *ever* slow down when a light turns yellow. If you're within half a block of a stoplight when it turns yellow, put the pedal to the metal.

When attempting to enter a street from any parking lot, make sure that at least the front third of your car is sticking out into the nearest lane.

When it starts raining, completely lose your ability to drive and act as if you've never done it before.

Using your turn signals is absolutely prohibited except in limited circumstances, such as when you're five feet from the corner. Never use your signal when you're making a right turn and someone is waiting to pull out into your lane.

A red light is not *truly* red until five seconds after the yellow light goes out.

BLOOPER

The women's prayer group held its annual salad supper. Beverly Hild's hot chick salad was the hit of the evening.

QUOTE

The depressing thing about tennis is that no matter how good I get, I will never be as good as a wall.

·DAY·
252 Each Friday night after work, Bubba would fire up his outdoor grill and cook thick steaks. But all of Bubba's neighbors were Catholic, and since it was Lent, they were forbidden from eating red meat on Friday.

The delicious aroma from the grilled steaks was causing such a problem for the Catholic faithful that they finally talked to their priest. The priest came to visit Bubba and suggested that he become a Catholic.

After several classes and much study, Bubba attended Mass. The priest sprinkled holy water over him and said, "You were born a Baptist and raised a Baptist, but now you are Catholic."

Bubba's neighbors were greatly relieved, until Friday night arrived and the wonderful aroma of grilled steak filled the neighborhood. The neighbors immediately called the priest.

As the priest rushed into Bubba's yard, clutching a rosary and prepared to scold him, he stopped and watched in amazement.

There stood Bubba, clutching a small bottle of holy water, which he carefully sprinkled over the grilling meat while chanting, "You wuz born a cow and raised a cow, but now you are a catfish."

BLOOPER

Mark Sunday, September 1, after church, on your calendars. This will be a time to eat and greet the new candidates for elder.

QUOTE

I haven't reported my missing credit cards to the police because whoever stole them is spending less than my wife.

· DAY · 253

When a mother returned from the grocery store, her small son pulled out the box of animal crackers he had begged for and spread the crackers all over the kitchen counter.

"What are you doing?" his mom asked.

"The box says you can't eat them if the seal is broken," the boy explained. "I'm looking for the seal."

BLOOPER

Representative Wilson asked, "Why have we do public schools?"

QUOTE

Never be afraid to try something new. Remember, amateurs built Noah's ark. Professionals built the *Titanic*.

· DAY · 254

A pickpocket was appearing in court for a series of petty crimes. "Mr. Brewster," the judge said, "you are hereby found guilty and fined a sum of $150."

After consulting with his client, Mr. Brewster's lawyer stood up and said, "Your Honor, my client is a little short at this time. He has only $125 in his pocket, but if you would allow him a few minutes in the crowd . . ."

BLOOPER

The Presbyterian Church of the Master will hold an evening of scared music next Sunday, July 14.

QUOTE

There are three kinds of people— those who can count and those who can't.

255 Two boys were arguing when their teacher entered the room. The teacher asked, "Why are you arguing?"

One boy answered, "We found a ten-dollar bill and decided to give it to whoever tells the biggest lie."

"You should be ashamed of yourselves," the teacher said. "When I was your age, I didn't even know what a lie was."

The boys gave the ten dollars to the teacher.

BLOOPER

John Fredricks, a member of the Valley View Church older board, will be speaking next week at Men's Night Out.

QUOTE

A foolish man tells his wife to stop talking. A wise man tells her that her mouth is beautiful when her lips are closed.

256 My husband is always complaining about my inability to stay on a budget and about the costs of running the household in general. This has become worse since we had twins. Everything is double—clothes, food, pediatrician bills. Lately he has even been complaining about the amount of baby powder I've been using on the twins to prevent them from getting diaper rashes. I've had to remind him that . . . talc is cheap.

BLOOPER

Sermon title: "Winter Forecast—It Will Be Cold."

QUOTE

Every morning I get up and look through the *Forbes* list of the richest people in America. If I'm not on it, I go to work.—*Robert Orben*

257 The Sunday school teacher was carefully explaining the story of Elijah the prophet and the false prophets of Baal. She explained how Elijah built the altar, put wood on it, cut the bull in pieces, and laid it on the altar. Then Elijah commanded the people of Israel to fill four barrels with water and pour it over the altar. He had them do this three times.

"Now," the teacher said, "can anyone in the class tell me why the Lord would have Elijah pour water over the bull on the altar?"

A little girl in the back of the room waved her hand. "I know! I know!" she said. "To make the gravy!"

Definitions:

Badaptation: a bad movie version of a good book.

Carbage: the trash found in your automobile.

Faddict: someone who has to try every new trend that comes along.

Gabberflasted: the state of being speechless due to someone else talking too much.

Hackchoo: when you sneeze and cough at the same time.

Jobsolete: a position within a company that no longer exists.

Knewlyweds: second marriage for both.

Lamplify: turning on (or up) the lights within a room.

Nagivator: someone who assists with driving directions in an overly critical manner.

Obliment: an obligatory compliment.

Pestariffic: adjective describing a particularly pesty person.

Qcumbersome: a salad that contains too many cucumbers.

Testimoney: fees paid to expert witnesses.

Unbrella: an umbrella that the wind has turned inside out.

Wackajacky: very messed up.

Yawnese: the language of someone trying to speak while yawning.

DAY 259

My job as a land surveyor took me to a golf course that was expanding from nine holes to eighteen holes.

Using a machete to clear thick brush in an area I was mapping, I came upon a golf club that an irate player must have tossed away. It was in good condition, so I picked it up and continued on.

When I broke out of the brush onto a putting green, two golfers stared at me in awe. I had a machete in one hand and a golf club in the other, and behind me was a clear-cut swath leading out of the woods.

"There," one of the golfers said, "is a guy who hates to lose his ball!"

BLOOPER

Mom-and-daughter PJ night next Friday. Bring your favorite Mexican.

QUOTE

Only a fool argues with a skunk, a mule, or the cook.

DAY 260

The parents in our cycling group were discussing the subject of teenagers and their appetites. Most agreed that teenagers would eat anything, anywhere, and at any time. Some were concerned that such appetites made it hard to judge when you should feed them because they were always grazing.

A veteran parent of six children told us his method for judging the true hunger of teenagers: "I would hold up a piece of cold, cooked broccoli, and if they were jumping and snapping at it, I figured they were hungry enough to be fed."

BLOOPER

Cemetery Meat Raffle to benefit St. Joe's church cemetery plots.

QUOTE

Duct tape is like the Force. It has a light side, a dark side, and it holds the universe together.

DAY 261

A new missionary recruit went to Venezuela for the first time. He was struggling with the language and didn't understand a whole lot of what was going on. Intending to visit one of the local churches, he got lost and arrived late, so the church was already packed. The only pew left was in the front row.

So as not to make a fool of himself, he chose to imitate the man sitting next to him on the front pew. As they sang, the man clapped his hands, so the missionary recruit clapped too. When the man stood up to pray, the missionary stood up too. When the man sat down, he sat down.

During the preaching, the recruit didn't understand a thing. He just sat there and tried to look just like that man in the front pew. Then the preacher said some words that he didn't understand, and he saw the man next to him stand up. So he stood up too. Suddenly a hush fell over the entire congregation. A few people gasped. He looked around and saw that nobody else was standing, so he sat down.

After the service ended, the preacher stood at the door shaking the hands of those who were leaving. When the missionary recruit stretched out his hand to greet the preacher, the preacher said in English, "I take it you don't speak Spanish."

The missionary recruit replied, "No, I don't. It's that obvious?"

"Well, yes," the preacher said. "I announced that the Acosta family had a newborn baby boy, and would the proud father please stand up."

BLOOPER

Gilda Morris spoke to the group and said that there's nothing more exciting than seeing the world with your best friend's spouse.

QUOTE

I hope life isn't some big joke, because I don't get it.

·DAY·
262

While carpenters were working outside the old house I had just bought, I busied myself with indoor cleaning. I had just finished washing the floor when one of the workmen asked to use the bathroom.

With dismay I looked from his muddy boots to my newly scrubbed floors. "Just a minute," I said, thinking of a quick solution. "I'll put down newspapers."

"That's all right, lady," he responded. "I'm already trained."

BLOOPER

She is teaching Engish in China.

QUOTE

A man with one watch knows what time it is; a man with two watches is never quite sure. —*Lee Segall*

263 A woman's four-year-old daughter was attending her first performance of the Ice Capades. She was so mesmerized that she wouldn't budge from her seat even during intermission, watching the activity while the ice was cleaned.

At the end of the show, the girl exclaimed, "I know what I want to be when I grow up!"

The mother envisioned her on the ice in another fifteen years, starring in the Ice Capades as a princess.

She was brought back to earth when her daughter continued, "I want to be a Zamboni driver!"

BLOOPER

The St. Charles Canine Club will hold a flea market on Saturday in the church parking lot.

QUOTE

Believe those who are seeking the truth. Doubt those who find it.
—*Andre Gide*

264 More two-line humor:

What do farmers give their wives on Valentine's Day?
Hogs and kisses!

Do skunks celebrate Valentine's Day?
Sure, they're very scent-imental!

What did the paper clip say to the magnet on Valentine's Day?
"I find you very attractive."

What did the French chef give his wife for Valentine's Day?
A hug and a quiche!

What did one light bulb say to the other?
"I love you a whole watt!"

What did the bat say to his Valentine?
"You're fun to hang around with."

What did the elephant say to his Valentine?
"I love you a ton."

What would you get if you crossed a blonde with the god of love?
A stupid cupid!

Men's thesaurus:

"It's a guy thing."
Translated: "There is no rational thought pattern connected with it, and you have no chance at all of making it logical."

"Can I help with dinner?"
Translated: "Why isn't dinner already on the table?"

"Take a break, honey. You're working too hard."
Translated: "I can't hear the game over the vacuum cleaner."

"That's interesting, dear."
Translated: "Are you still talking?"

"Oh, don't fuss—I just cut myself. It's no big deal."
Translated: "I have actually severed a limb but will bleed to death before I admit that I'm hurt."

"I heard you."
Translated: "I haven't the foggiest clue what you just said and am hoping desperately that I can fake it well enough so that you don't spend the next three days yelling at me."

"You look terrific."
Translated: "Oh, please don't try on one more outfit. I'm starving."

"I'm not lost. I know exactly where we are."
Translated: "No one will ever see us alive again."

266

One day God was walking in the garden of Eden. After a short while, he came across Adam, who was in low spirits that particular day. God asked him what was wrong, and Adam told the Lord that he was lonely.

God responded that he would create a companion for Adam. She would walk by his side for all eternity. She would listen to his problems. She would wash his clothes. She would keep his house clean. She would cook his meals. She would do anything to keep him happy. Most importantly, she would never complain or nag him.

Adam was ecstatic. His spirits lifted immediately. The Lord hated to tell him that this creature would come at a price—she would cost him an arm and a leg.

Adam responded, "What can I get for a rib?"

And the rest is history.

BLOOPER

Brother Quinn, owner of the Magic Wok on Route 43, is now serving Chinese food.

QUOTE

Sometimes it is necessary to go a long distance out of the way in order to come back a short distance correctly.—*Edward Albee*

267

A man went to the police station wishing to speak with the burglar who had broken into his house the night before.

"You'll get your chance in court," the desk sergeant said.

"No, no, no!" the man said. "I want to know how he got into the house without waking my wife. I've been trying to do that for years!"

BLOOPER

Church school superintendent Horton said that increasing number of parents now opt to have their children school-homed.

QUOTE

By daily dying, I have come to be.
—*Theodore Roethke*

·DAY·
268

A couple was celebrating their fiftieth anniversary at the church's marriage marathon, so the minister asked Brother Ralph, the husband, to take a few minutes and share some insight into how he managed to live with the same woman all these years.

Ralph replied to the audience, "Well, I treated her with respect and spent money on her, but mostly I took her traveling on special occasions."

"To where?" the minister asked him.

"For our twenty-fifth anniversary, I took her to Beijing, China," Ralph replied.

"What a terrific example you are to all husbands, Ralph," the minister said. "Please tell the audience what you're going to do for your wife on your fiftieth anniversary."

Brother Ralph said, "I'm going back to get her."

BLOOPER

Kids under 2 eat free at the all-church supper—if accompanied by an adult.

QUOTE

You never know what is enough, until you know what is more than enough.—*William Blake*

·DAY·
269

The phone rang. It was a salesman from a mortgage refinance company. "Do you have a second mortgage on your home?" he asked.

"No," the woman replied.

"Would you like to consolidate all your debts?"

"I really don't have any," she said.

"How about freeing up cash for home improvements?" he continued.

"I don't need any. I just recently had some done and paid cash," she said.

There was a brief silence, and then he asked, "Are you looking for a husband?"

BLOOPER

An evening of mucus and fellowship will follow. Bring a blanket and sit on the lawn.

QUOTE

What you can see, yet cannot see over, is as good as infinite.—*Thomas Carlyle*

· DAY ·
270

One night while I was cat-sitting my daughter's indoor feline, it escaped outside. When it failed to return the following morning, I found the cat clinging to a branch about thirty feet up in a spindly tree. Unable to lure it down, I called the fire department.

"We don't do that anymore," the woman dispatcher said. When I persisted, she was polite but firm. "The cat will come down when it gets hungry enough."

"How do you know that?" I asked.

"Have you ever seen a cat skeleton in a tree?"

Two hours later the cat was back, looking for breakfast.

BLOOPER

Except for the arsenic levels, the church drinking water was rated as safe to drink.

QUOTE

Think like a man of action, act like a man of thought.—*Henri Louis Bergson*

· DAY ·
271

One night a wife found her husband standing over their baby's crib. Silently she watched him. As he stood looking down at the sleeping infant, she saw on his face a mixture of emotions: disbelief, doubt, delight, amazement, enchantment, skepticism.

Touched by this unusual display, with eyes glistening she slipped her arm around her husband.

"A penny for your thoughts," she said.

"It's amazing!" he replied. "I just can't see how anybody can make a crib like that for only $46.50."

BLOOPER

Elder Johns said that his sinning lessons are now available online.

QUOTE

Don't miss the donut by looking through the hole.

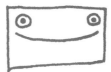

Two buddies, Bob and Earl, were two of the biggest baseball fans in America. For their entire adult lives, Bob and Earl discussed baseball history in the winter and pored over every box score during the season. They went to sixty games a year. They even agreed that whoever died first would try to come back and tell the other if there was baseball in heaven.

One summer night, Bob passed away in his sleep after watching the Yankee victory earlier in the evening. He died happy. A few nights later, his buddy Earl awoke to the sound of Bob's voice from beyond.

"Bob, is that you?" Earl asked.

"Of course it's me," Bob replied.

"This is unbelievable!" Earl exclaimed. "So tell me, is there baseball in heaven?"

"Well, I have some good news and some bad news for you. Which do you want to hear first?"

"Tell me the good news first."

"Well, the good news is that, yes, there is baseball in heaven, Earl."

"Oh, that is wonderful! So what could possibly be the bad news?"

"You're pitching tomorrow night."

BLOOPER

Sister Florence Dent hit a moose on her way to visit her sister who hit a moose.

QUOTE

You can't wake a person who is pretending to be asleep.

"Ever since we got married, my wife has tried to change me," a man said to his friend. "She got me to stop drinking, smoking, and running around until all hours of the night. She taught me how to dress well, enjoy the fine arts, appreciate gourmet cooking and classical music, and even invest in the stock market."

"Sounds like you may be bitter because she changed you so drastically," his friend remarked.

"I'm not bitter. Now that I'm so improved, she just isn't good enough for me."

BLOOPER

Our Women's Hacienda Night will feature tacos with found beef and salsa.

QUOTE

If you chase two rabbits, you will not catch either one.—*Russian proverb*

274

Last year I entered the New York City marathon. The race started, and immediately I was the last of the runners. It was embarrassing.

The guy who was in front of me, second to last, was making fun of me. He said, "Hey, buddy, how does it feel to be last?"

I replied, "You really want to know?"

Then I dropped out of the race.

BLOOPER

Pastor Evans said that all eating disorders seem to be directly linked in some way to food.

QUOTE

Some people walk in the rain, others just get wet.—*Roger Miller*

275

Five surgeons are discussing the best patients to operate on. The first surgeon says, "I like to see accountants on my operating table, because when you open them up, everything inside is numbered."

The second responds, "Yeah, but you should try electricians! Everything inside them is color-coded."

The third surgeon says, "No, I really think file clerks are the best; everything inside them is in alphabetical order."

The fourth surgeon chimes in, "You know, I like construction workers. Those guys always understand when you have a few parts left over at the end and when the job takes longer than you said it would."

But the fifth surgeon shuts them all up when he observes, "You're all wrong. Politicians are the easiest to operate on. There are no guts, no heart, and no spine, and the head and tail are interchangeable."

BLOOPER

The elders are debating methods that they could use to fix elections in the future.

QUOTE

It is better to know some of the questions than all of the answers.—*James Thurber*

Sister Mary, who worked for a home health agency, was out making her rounds visiting homebound patients when she ran out of gas. As luck would have it, a gas station was just a block away.

She walked to the station to borrow a gas can and buy some gas. The attendant told her that the only gas can he owned had been lent out, but she could wait until it was returned.

Since the nun was on the way to see a patient, she decided not to wait and walked back to her car. She looked for something in her car that she could fill with gas and spotted the bedpan she was taking to the patient. Always resourceful, she carried the bedpan to the station, filled it with gas, and took it back to her car.

As she was pouring the gas into her tank, two men watched from across the street. One of them turned to the other and said, "If it starts, I'm turning Catholic."

BLOOPER

Vendors at our Health Fest will be selling hot dogs, donuts, corn dogs, candy, and a whole lot more.

QUOTE

It is easy to stand a pain, but difficult to stand an itch.

A mother mouse and a baby mouse are walking along when all of a sudden a cat attacks them. The mother mouse yells, "Woof!" and the cat runs away.

"See?" the mother mouse says to her baby. "Now do you understand why it's important to learn a foreign language?"

BLOOPER

The Open Door Church was entered by unknown people by breaking a window. Nothing was reported missing.

QUOTE

What deep wounds ever closed without a scar?—*Lord Byron*

DAY 278

All I need to know about life I learned from a snowman:

It's okay if you're a little bottom-heavy.

Hold your ground, even when the heat is on.

Wearing white is always appropriate.

Winter is the best of the four seasons.

It takes a few extra rolls to make a good midsection.

There's nothing better than a foul-weather friend.

The key to life is to be a jolly, happy soul.

We're all made up of mostly water.

You know you've made it when they write a song about you.

Accessorize! Accessorize! Accessorize!

Avoid yellow snow.

Don't get too much sun.

Don't be embarrassed when you can't look down and see your feet.

It's fun to hang out in your front yard.

There's no stopping you once you're on a roll.

BLOOPER

Optimist Club, which meets at our church on Thursday, is going better than they expected.

QUOTE

Tomorrow always comes and today is never yesterday.—*S. A. Sachs*

DAY 279

Customer call center blues:

Customer: "I've been ringing 0700-2300 for two days and can't get through to enquiries. Can you help?"

Operator: "Where did you get that number from, sir?"

Customer: "It was on the door to the travel center."

Operator: "Sir, those are our operating hours."

Caller: "I deleted a file from my PC last week, and I just realized that I need it. If I turn my system clock back two weeks, will I have my file back again?"

Customer: "Can you give me the telephone number for Jack?"

Operator: "I'm sorry, sir, I don't understand who you're talking about."

Customer: "On page 1, section 5, of the user guide, it clearly states that I need to unplug the fax machine from the AC wall socket and telephone Jack before cleaning. Now, can you give me the number for Jack?"

Operator: "I think you mean the telephone socket on the wall."

Directory Assistance Calls

Caller: "I'd like the number of Ill's Grill in Wilsonville, Illinois."

Operator: "I'm sorry, but there's no listing. Is the spelling correct?"

Caller: "Well, it used to be called Bill's Grill, but the 'B' fell off."

BLOOPER

Church bulletin board—For sale: Beautiful wedding dress—5'7" wide, 7'2" long.

QUOTE

Weak eyes are fondest of glittering objects.—*Thomas Carlyle*

280

Unanswerable questions:

Do you think sheep know when you're pulling the wool over their eyes?

Does the person who inventories sheep often fall asleep on the job?

If a pig is sold to the pawn shop, is it called a ham hock?

If we make sweaters out of sheep's hair, what do sheep use to make sweaters?

If you pushed a pig down a hill, would it be a sausage roll?

What do pigs say when they don't want to do something? Would it be "Yeah, when humans fly"?

What do sheep count when they can't get to sleep?

Why do pigs have curly tails?

Why do we call them guinea pigs when they are neither from Guinea nor are pigs?

Why don't sheep shrink when it rains?

Why is it that the first thing we try to do after killing a pig is to cure it?

Would a small pig be called a hamlet?

BLOOPER

Church bulletin board—found: Large white poodle resembling a dog.

QUOTE

You can see a lot by just looking.—*Yogi Berra*

281

Deciphering the doctor:

What the doctor says: "This should be taken care of right away."
What the doctor is thinking: *I'd planned a trip to Hawaii next month, but this is so easy and profitable that I want to fix it before it cures itself.*

"Wellllll, what have we here?"
I have no idea and am hoping you'll give me a clue.

"Let me check your medical history."
I want to see if you've paid your last bill before spending any more time with you.

"We have some good news and some bad news."
The good news is, I'm going to buy that new BMW. The bad news is, you're going to pay for it.

"Let's see how it develops."
Maybe in a few days it will grow into something that can be cured.

"Why don't we make another appointment later in the week."
I'm playing golf this afternoon, and this is a waste of time. Plus I need the bucks, so I'm charging you for another office visit.

"Let me schedule you for some tests."
I have a 40 percent interest in the lab.

"I'd like to prescribe a new drug."
I'm writing a paper and would like to use you for a guinea pig.

BLOOPER

The church's workshop on openness is now closed.

QUOTE

Sometimes the questions are complicated and the answers simple.—*Dr. Seuss*

·DAY· 282

A fellow was walking along a country road when he came upon a farmer working in his field. The man called out to the farmer, "How long will it take me to get to the next town?"

The farmer didn't answer. The guy waited a bit and then started walking again.

After the man had gone about a hundred yards, the farmer yelled out, "About twenty minutes."

"Thank you. But why didn't you tell me that when I first asked you?"

"Didn't know how fast you could walk."

BLOOPER

The Sunday school class felt like it was in 1942—when they visited a replica of the *Niña* and the *Pinta* at the yacht harbor.

QUOTE

When the pain is great enough, we will let anyone be doctor.—*Mignon McLaughlin*

Billy's birthday was coming up, and he thought this was a good time to tell his mother what he wanted. "Mom, I want a bike for my birthday."

Billy could be a bit of a troublemaker, so his mother asked him if he thought he deserved to get a bike for his birthday.

"Of course," he said.

Billy's mother, a religious woman, replied, "Go to your room, Billy, and think about how you've behaved this year. Then write a letter to God and tell him why you deserve a bike for your birthday."

Billy stomped up the steps to his room and sat down to write God a letter.

Letter 1: "Dear God, I have been a very good boy this year, and I would like a bike for my birthday. I want a red one. Your friend, William."

Billy knew he was telling a pretty big fib, so he tore the letter up and wrote a new one.

Letter 2: "Dear God, I have been an okay boy this year. I still would like a bike for my birthday. Billy."

This letter was no good either.

Letter 3: "Dear God, I know I haven't been a good boy this year. I am very sorry, and I will be a good boy next year if you just send me a bike for my birthday. Please. Thank you. Billy."

Billy knew this wasn't true either, and now he was getting upset. He went downstairs and told his mother he needed to go to church. She thought her plan had worked and told him to be home in time for dinner.

Billy walked into the church and went to the altar. He looked around to see if anyone was watching, then picked up a statue of the Virgin Mary and slipped it under his coat.

Letter 4: "Dear God, I got your mama. If you want to see her again, send the bike. Signed, You Know Who."

BLOOPER

The Seniors for Lunch group will be hosting meatless Mondays on Tuesdays now.

QUOTE

The scars you can't see are the hardest to heal.—*Astrid Alauda*

As we were driving to school today, my seven-year-old said, "I want to hear 'Back in Black'" (from one of the *Men in Black* soundtracks).

"No, I'm in the mood for something classical," I said.

"But I don't want Mozart," she replied.

"How about Rachmaninov?" I suggested, but she remained silent.

The Best of Rachmaninov started playing, and she objected, "I said I don't want to hear Mozart."

"It's not Mozart—it's Rachmaninov," I said.

"Well," she said indignantly, "I don't hear the 'rock' part."

BLOOPER

Todd Besterly has two burial plots for sale. Great location. Slightly used.

QUOTE

Almost every wise saying has an opposite one, no less wise, to balance it.—*Santayana*

285

A young woman was about to finish her first year of college. She considered herself to be a very liberal Democrat, but her father was a rather staunch Republican.

One day she was challenging her father on his beliefs and his opposition to taxes and welfare programs. He stopped her and asked how she was doing in school.

She answered that she had a 4.0 GPA, but it was really tough. She had to study all the time, and she never had time to go out and party. She didn't have time for a boyfriend and didn't really have many college friends because of spending all her time studying.

He asked, "How is your friend Mary?" She replied that Mary was barely getting by. She had a 2.0 GPA and never studied. She was very popular on campus and went to parties all the time. She often didn't show up for classes because she was hung over.

Dad then asked his daughter why she didn't go to the dean's office and have 1.0 taken off her 4.0 and give it to her friend with the 2.0. That way they would both have a 3.0 GPA.

The daughter angrily fired back, "That wouldn't be fair! I worked really hard for my grades, and Mary has done nothing."

The father slowly smiled and said, "Welcome to the Republican party."

BLOOPER

Bishop Ford explained that if it hadn't rained, the roof would not have leaked.

QUOTE

Our greatest pretenses are built up not to hide the evil and the ugly in us, but our emptiness. The hardest thing to hide is something that is not there.—*Eric Hoffer*

286

Golf truisms:

I don't say my golf game is bad, but if I grew tomatoes, they'd come up sliced.

I've spent most of my life golfing. The rest I've just wasted.

Golf is played by twenty million American men whose wives think they are out having fun.

Golf is a game in which you yell "fore," shoot six, and write down five.

Give me golf clubs, fresh air, and a beautiful partner, and you can keep the clubs and the fresh air.

The only time my prayers are never answered is on the golf course.

Reverse every natural instinct and do the opposite of what you are inclined to do, and you will probably come very close to having a perfect golf swing.

If you think it's hard to meet new people, try picking up the wrong golf ball.

It's good sportsmanship not to pick up lost golf balls while they are still rolling.

The difference in golf and government is that in golf you can't improve your lie.

Golf is a game invented by the same people who think music comes out of a bagpipe.

BLOOPER

Pastor Peter picked as Parish Pastor of the Year.

QUOTE

What is more foolish, the child afraid of the dark, or the man afraid of the light?—*Maurice Freehill*

The young woman really thought she'd been very patient through a protracted period of dating with no talk of marriage.

One night her steady boyfriend took her to a Chinese restaurant. As he perused the menu, he casually asked her, "So, how do you like your rice? Steamed or fried?"

Without missing a beat, she looked over her menu at him and replied, "Thrown."

BLOOPER

Church bulletin board: Naughty pine furniture for sale.

QUOTE

An egg cannot be unscrambled.
—*American proverb*

·DAY· 288

A woman phoned her dentist when she received a huge bill. "I'm shocked!" she said. "This is three times what you normally charge."

"Yes, I know," the dentist said. "But you yelled so loud, you scared away two other patients."

BLOOPER

The elders have said that sex education is on the table.

QUOTE

Admiration and familiarity are strangers.—*George Sand*

·DAY· 289

From papers written by a class of eight-year-olds:

Grandparents are a lady and a man who have no little children of their own. They like other people's.

Grandparents don't have to do anything except be there when we come to see them. They are so old they shouldn't play hard or run. They show us and talk to us about the color of the flowers and also why we shouldn't step on cracks.

They don't say, "Hurry up."

Usually grandmothers are fat, but not too fat to tie your shoes.

Everybody should try to have a grandmother, especially if you don't have television, because they are the only grown-ups who like to spend time with us.

Grandparents wear glasses and funny underwear.

They can take their teeth and gums out.

When they read to us, they don't skip. They don't mind if we ask for the same story over again.

They know we should have snack time before bedtime, and they say prayers with us every time, and they kiss us even when we've been bad.

BLOOPER	QUOTE
The denominational headquarters is looking for job applicants for supervisor: men or women only.	To know the height of a mountain, one must climb it.—*Augustus William Hare*

· DAY · 290

Mom and I returned home late one evening, so my father, my college-age brother, Steven, and my ten-year-old sister were asleep.

Mom had forgotten her house keys, so we knocked loudly, first at the back door and then the front and side doors. We yelled my father's name over and over, with no answer. The car horn aroused the neighbors but no one at our house. We drove into town and phoned home, finally waking Steven.

When we got back, he let us in. Dad was in bed, snoring, with the television on. Mom quietly switched it off, and Dad woke right up.

"Don't turn that off," he said. "I'm watching it!"

BLOOPER	QUOTE
Brother Felger, owner of Bob's Burgers, is offering $1 double melts to all members—limit 500.	No snowflake ever falls in the wrong place.

DAY 291

Golf truisms:

If you want to hit a 7-iron as far as Tiger Woods does, simply try to lay up just short of a water hazard.

There are two things you can learn by stopping your backswing at the top and checking the position of your hands: how many hands you have, and which one is wearing the glove.

A two-foot putt counts the same as a two-foot drive.

It's a simple matter to keep your ball in the fairway if you're not too choosy about which fairway.

Hazards attract; fairways repel.

For most golfers, the only difference between a one-dollar ball and a three-dollar ball is two dollars.

You can put "draw" on the ball, you can put "fade" on the ball, but no golfer can put "straight" on the ball.

An extra ball in the pocket is worth two strokes in the bush.

A ball you can see in the rough from fifty yards away is not yours.

If there is a ball in the fringe and a ball in the bunker, your ball is in the bunker.

If both balls are in the bunker, yours is in the footprint.

Don't buy a putter until you've had a chance to throw it.

BLOOPER

Church bulletin board—For sale: Feeding trough, galvanized. Can be used for pigs or for baptizing.

QUOTE

I've observed that there are more lines formed than things worth waiting for.—*Robert Brault*

DAY 292

Soon after our high-tech company moved into a new building, we had trouble with the elevators. A manager got stuck between floors and, after some door banging, finally attracted attention. His name was taken and rescue promised.

It took two hours before the elevator mechanic arrived and got the manager out. When he returned to his desk, he found this note from his efficient secretary: "The elevator people called and will be here in two hours."

BLOOPER

Neighbor notes: A cow from Tom Ke-mer's farm was struck and killed by the milk truck.

QUOTE

Genuine tragedies in the world are not conflicts between right and wrong. They are conflicts between two rights.—*George Hegel*

Things I learned:

I learned that I like my teacher because she cries when we sing "Silent Night."—Age 5

I learned that although it's hard to admit it, I'm secretly glad my parents are strict with me.—Age 15

I learned that wherever I go, the world's worst drivers have followed me there.—Age 29

I learned that there are people who love you dearly but just don't know how to show it.—Age 42

I learned that the greater a person's sense of guilt, the greater his or her need to cast blame on others.—Age 46

I learned that you can tell a lot about a man by the way he handles these three things: a rainy day, lost luggage, and tangled Christmas tree lights.—Age 51

I learned that regardless of your relationship with your parents, you miss them terribly after they die.—Age 53

I learned that making a living is not the same thing as making a life.—Age 58

I learned that if you want to do something positive for your children, work to improve your marriage.—Age 61

I learned that everyone can use a prayer.—Age 72

I learned that even when I have pains, I don't have to be one.—Age 82

I learned that I still have a lot to learn.—Age 92

BLOOPER

The Charlestown singles class wel-comes singles of all ages—widowed, divorced, or married.

QUOTE

To believe with certainty, we must begin with doubting.—*Stanislaus I of Poland*

294 Insightful insights:

> One time a cop pulled me over for running a stop sign. He said, "Didn't you see the stop sign?" and I said, "Yeah, but I don't believe everything I read."
>
> The other day, I was walking my dog around my building—on the ledge. . . . Some people are afraid of heights. Not me. I'm afraid of widths.
>
> There's a fine line between fishing and standing on the shore looking like an idiot.
>
> Today I met with a subliminal advertising executive for just a second.
>
> What's another word for *thesaurus*?
>
> When I woke up this morning, my wife asked me, "Did you sleep good?" I said, "No, I made a few mistakes."
>
> Why is the alphabet in that order? Is it because of that song?
>
> You can't have everything. Where would you put it?
>
> You know how it is when you go to be the subject of a psychology experiment and nobody else shows up, and you think maybe that's part of the experiment? I'm like that all the time.
>
> You know how it is when you're walking up the stairs and you get to the top, and you think there's one more step? I'm like that all the time.

BLOOPER

Sister July Young is looking for a new manurist for her spa.

QUOTE

A wise man sees more from the bottom of a well than a fool from a mountain-top.

295 Insightful insights:

> Babies don't need a vacation, but I still see them at the beach. It ticks me off! I'll go over to a little baby and say, "What are you doing here? You haven't worked a day in your life!"
>
> Do you think that when they asked George Washington for ID, he just whipped out a quarter?
>
> Ever notice how irons have a setting for *permanent* press? I don't get it.
>
> For my birthday I got a humidifier and a dehumidifier. I put them in the same room and let them fight it out.

I bought some used paint. It was in the shape of a house.

I collect rare photographs—I have two. One is of Houdini locking his keys in his car. The other is of Norman Rockwell beating up a child.

I have a hobby—I have the world's largest collection of seashells. I keep it scattered on beaches all over the world. Maybe you've seen some of it.

I have an existential map. It has "You are here" written all over it.

I installed a skylight in my apartment. The people who live above me are furious!

I just bought a microwave fireplace. You can spend an evening in front of it in only eight minutes.

I put a new engine in my car but didn't take the old one out. Now my car goes five hundred miles an hour.

I spilled spot remover on my dog and now he's gone.

BLOOPER

The elder board has some disagreement with agreement they never agreed to.

QUOTE

A stumble may prevent a fall.
—*English proverb*

Abe came home one day and found his wife, Esther, in tears. "Darling, what's the matter?"

"Oh, Abe," Esther cried, "Doctor Cohen says I have tuberculosis."

"What! A big healthy woman like you has tuberculosis? Ridiculous," Abe said. "I'll call Doctor Cohen and get this sorted out right now."

So Abe called the doctor. "Doctor, Esther says you told her she has tuberculosis."

The doctor said something to Abe, who began laughing.

"What's so funny about my having such a dreadful disease?" Esther asked.

"Esther, Doctor Cohen didn't say you have tuberculosis, he said you have 'too big a tushas'!"

BLOOPER

Stones for Eternity is offering a pre—Mother's Day sale on headstones.

QUOTE

Do not seek to follow in the footsteps of a wise man. Seek what the wise man sought.

·DAY·

297
The following are actual medical records taken from patients' charts around North America:

The baby was delivered, the cord clamped and cut and handed to the pediatrician, who breathed and cried immediately.

The patient was in his usual state of good health until his airplane ran out of gas and crashed.

I saw your patient today, who is still under our car for physical therapy.

The patient lives at home with his mother, father, and pet turtle, who is presently enrolled in day care three times a week.

She is numb from her toes down.

While in the emergency room, she was examined, X-rated, and sent home.

Occasional, constant, infrequent headaches.

Patient was alert and unresponsive.

When she fainted, her eyes rolled around the room.

BLOOPER

Remember, the church employee parking lot is for parking two hours or less.

QUOTE

The world is round, and the place which may seem like the end may also be only the beginning.—*Ivy Baker Priest*

Homework excuses:

> I didn't do my history homework because I don't believe in dwelling on the past.
>
> I didn't want the other kids in the class to look bad.
>
> Our furnace broke, and we had to burn my homework to keep ourselves from freezing.
>
> I'm not at liberty to say why.
>
> I have a solar-powered calculator, and it was cloudy.
>
> I made a paper plane out of it and it got hijacked.
>
> My agent won't allow me to publish my homework until the movie deal is finalized.
>
> It's against my religion to do any homework.
>
> I felt it wasn't challenging enough.
>
> My parents were sick and unable to do my homework last night. Don't worry, they have been suitably punished.
>
> We had homework?!
>
> I see your lips moving, but all I'm hearing is "blah, blah, blah."
>
> I spent the night at a rally supporting higher pay for our hard-working teachers.

BLOOPER

Elder care activities: Tuesday is "Who Am I" Day.

QUOTE

People who look through keyholes are apt to get the idea that most things are keyhole shaped.

· DAY ·
299

Student answers:

Teacher: It's clear that you haven't studied your geography. What's your excuse?

Student: Well, my dad says the world is changing every day. So I decided to wait until it settles down!

Teacher: Why are you always late for school?

Student: Because you always ring the bell before I get here!

Teacher: What are the small rivers that run into the Nile?

Student: The juve-niles!

Teacher: What are the Great Plains?

Student: A 747, a Concorde, and an F-16.

Teacher: Where is the English Channel?

Student: I don't know—my TV doesn't pick it up.

Teacher: Why does the Statue of Liberty stand in the New York Harbor?

Student: Because it can't sit down!

Teacher: Is Lapland heavily populated?

Student: No, there are not many Lapps to the mile!

Teacher: Name an animal that lives in Lapland.

Student: A reindeer.

Teacher: Good, now name another.

Student: Another reindeer!

BLOOPER

Cathy Rostow discussed the recent church sex survey: teens are active but uniformed.

QUOTE

A real patriot is the fellow who gets the parking ticket and rejoices that the system works.—*Bill Vaughn*

The judge admonished the witness, "Do you understand that you have sworn to tell the truth?"

"I do."

"Do you understand what will happen if you are not truthful?"

"Sure," the witness said. "My side will win."

BLOOPER

Due to the picketing by our church, the Lion's Den strip club will be given ten years to shut down.

QUOTE

If you are being run out of town, get in front of the mob and make it look like a parade.

While watching a movie recently, I couldn't hear the dialogue over the chatter of the two women sitting in front of me. Unable to bear it any longer, I tapped one of them on the shoulder.

"Excuse me," I said, "I can't hear."

"I should hope not," she replied sharply. "This is a private conversation."

BLOOPER

St. Paul's neurosurgery department gets a new head.

QUOTE

Do not call any work menial until you have watched a proud person do it.

302

An old man was sitting on his porch when a young man walked up with a pad and pencil in his hand.

"What are you selling, young man?" he asked.

"I'm not selling anything, sir," the young man replied. "I'm a census taker."

"A what?" the man asked.

"A census taker. We're trying to find out how many people are in the United States."

"Well," the man answered, "you're wasting your time with me; I have no idea."

BLOOPER

Lord to speak to CC Christian Women's Club.

QUOTE

We judge others by their behavior. We judge ourselves by our intentions.
—Ian Percy

303

One of my first assignments as a trainee in an auto body shop was a car needing a new fender and some door repairs.

I spent hours doing a perfect job, but when the owner came to pick it up, he wasn't pleased.

"What's wrong?" I asked.

Pointing to the side of the car, he complained about the paint not matching, uneven gaps between panels, and a host of other problems. He demanded an explanation.

I said, "The repairs were to the other side."

BLOOPER

Jewish Federation honors Bacon.

QUOTE

The moment one gives close attention to anything, even a blade of grass, it becomes a mysterious, awesome, indescribably magnificent world in itself.—*Henry Miller*

I know I'm not going to understand women. I'll never understand how you can take boiling hot wax, pour it onto your upper thigh, rip the hair out by the root, and still be afraid of a spider.

BLOOPER

Doctor Hillings said that if you are 100 pounds overweight, you should make an appointment for next week. If your heart stops beating, you should call the doctor immediately.

QUOTE

There is no such thing as bragging. Either you're telling the truth or you're not.—*Al Oliver*

305 More unanswerable questions:

Why does a round pizza come in a square box?

Why is it that people say they "slept like a baby" when babies wake up like every two hours?

Why do people pay to go up tall buildings and then put money in binoculars to look at things on the ground?

Why do toasters always have a setting that burns the toast to a horrible crisp, which no decent human being would eat?

If Jimmy cracks corn and no one cares, why is there a stupid song about him?

Can a hearse carrying a corpse drive in the carpool lane?

If the professor on *Gilligan's Island* can make a radio out of a coconut, why can't he fix a hole in a boat?

Why does Goofy stand up straight while Pluto remains on all fours? They're both dogs!

If Wile E. Coyote had enough money to buy all that Acme stuff, why didn't he just buy dinner?

If corn oil is made from corn and vegetable oil is made from vegetables, what is baby oil made from?

Do the alphabet song and "Twinkle, Twinkle, Little Star" have the same tune?

Why did you just try singing the two songs above?

BLOOPER

Good news for troubled parents: children are not likely to inherit your infertility.

QUOTE

A penny will hide the biggest star in the universe if you hold it close enough to your eye.—*Samuel Grafton*

A mother was dropping her son off at a friend's house. She said to him, "Will you be good while Mommy's gone?"

"If you give me a dollar!" the boy replied.

His mother shook her head and said to him, "Why can't you be good for nothing like your father?"

BLOOPER

Our church school teachers have requested that the elder board not lower eduction bar any lower.

QUOTE

Is the glass half empty, half full, or twice as large as it needs to be?

One Sunday morning, while stationed at Osan Air Base in South Korea, I was in line for breakfast and noticed that the cook behind the counter looked kind of harassed. After I gave him my order, he asked me how I wanted my eggs.

Not wanting to burden him further, I said cheerfully, "Oh, whatever is easiest for you."

With that, he took two eggs, cracked them open onto my plate, and handed it back to me.

BLOOPER

Church member Dr. Reedy said that when it comes to colonoscopies, location matters.

QUOTE

Don't think of organ donations as giving up part of yourself to keep a total stranger alive. It's really a total stranger giving up almost all of themselves to keep part of you alive.

DAY 308

Old Abraham was a poor tailor whose shop was next door to a very upscale French restaurant. Every day at lunchtime, Abraham would go outside his shop and eat his black bread and herring while smelling the wonderful odors coming from the restaurant's kitchen.

One day, Abraham was surprised to receive an invoice from the restaurant for "enjoyment of food." So he went to the restaurant to point out that he had not bought anything from them. The manager told him, "You're enjoying our food, so you should pay us for it."

Abraham refused to pay, and the restaurant sued him. At the hearing, the judge asked the restaurant manager to present his side of the case. The manager said, "Every day, this man comes and sits outside our kitchen and smells our food while eating his. It is clear that we are providing added value to his poor food, and we deserve to be compensated for it."

The judge turned to Abraham and said, "What do you have to say?"

Abraham didn't say anything but stuck his hand in his pocket and rattled the few coins he had.

"What is the meaning of that?" the judge asked.

Abraham replied, "I'm paying for the smell of his food with the sound of my money."

BLOOPER

Overeaters Anonymous at St. Joseph's Parish hall. Drive to the back of the building and park near the dumpsters. Please use the double-door entrance.

QUOTE

Be careful how you interpret the world. Whatever you see, it will be like that.—*Erich Heller*

DAY 309

A lifeguard told a mother to make her young son stop urinating in the pool.

"Everyone knows," the mother said, "that from time to time, young children will urinate in a pool."

"Oh really?" the lifeguard said. "From the diving board?"

BLOOPER

Do you choose to share in the cup at communion? If so, you might be aware that it has come to our attention that some individuals are "gulping" from the cup, rather than "sipping" from the cup. The cups we use are small containers, so they can be emptied quickly if recipients drink more than a sip. At the same time, however, there is no objection if you are near the end of the communion line and if there is still a fairly large amount of the precious blood in the cup. Thanks, the Communion Committee.

QUOTE

The aim of an argument or discussion should not be victory, but progress.

· DAY ·
310

My friend's big church wedding was fast approaching, and she was delighted to hear that her mom, who had emerged from a nasty divorce, had finally found the perfect mother-of-the-bride dress.

Two days later, the bride was shocked to learn that her new young stepmother had purchased the same dress. My friend asked her stepmother to buy another dress since her mom had already altered her purchase. Her stepmother refused.

After two more weeks of frustrating shopping, the bride's mom found a dress that was not as nice as the first but would serve. When asked by a friend what she would do with her original dress, she grinned and replied, "I'm wearing it to the rehearsal dinner!"

BLOOPER

Circus Court Judge Mendenhall to speak to men's group.

QUOTE

The guy who invented the first wheel was an idiot. The guy who invented the other three, he was a genius.
—*Sid Caesar*

·DAY·

311

An elderly woman had just returned to her home from an evening church service when she was startled by an intruder. She caught the man in the act of robbing her home of its valuables and yelled, "Stop! Acts 2:38!" ("Repent and be baptized, every one of you, in the name of Jesus Christ for the forgiveness of your sins.")

The burglar stopped in his tracks. The woman calmly called the police and explained what she had done. As the officer cuffed the man to take him in, he asked the burglar, "Why did you just stand there? All the old lady did was yell a Scripture to you."

"Scripture?" the burglar replied. "She said she had an ax and two 38s!"

BLOOPER

The new health clinic in Middleburg will offer impatient and outpatient therapy.

QUOTE

If you wish to make an apple pie truly from scratch, you must first invent the universe.

·DAY·

312

Tot truisms:

Melanie (age five) asked her granny how old she was. Granny replied she was so old she didn't remember anymore. Melanie said, "If you don't remember, look in the back of your panties. Mine say five to six."

Di (age four) stepped onto the bathroom scale and asked, "How much do I cost?"

Marc (age four) was engrossed with a young man and woman who were hugging and kissing in a restaurant. Without taking his eyes off them, he asked his dad, "Why is he whispering in her mouth?"

Clinton (age five) was in his bedroom looking worried. When his mom asked what was troubling him, he replied, "I don't know what'll happen with this bed when I get married. How will my wife fit in?"

James (age four) was listening to a Bible story. His dad read, "The man named Lot was warned to take his wife and flee out of the city, but his wife looked back and was turned to salt." Concerned, James asked, "What happened to the flea?"

Tammy (age four) was with her mother when they met an elderly, rather wrinkled woman her mom knew. Tammy looked at her for a while and then asked, "Why doesn't your skin fit your face?"

BLOOPER

Adult video Sunday school meets in room 210.

QUOTE

There is no burnt rice to a hungry person.—*Philippine proverb*

·DAY·
313

Bumper stickers:

Don't play stupid with me . . . I'm better at it!

This car is designed by a computer, built by a robot, driven by a moron.

This truck has been in 15 accidents . . . and hasn't lost one yet.

Faster than a speeding ticket.

Adults are just kids with money.

T.G.I.F. Thank God I'm Female.

You are right where you belong, behind me!

They keep saying the right person will come along; I think a bus hit mine.

Reality is a nice place, but I wouldn't want to live there.

Was today really necessary?

In theory, everything works.

Death is life's way of telling you you're fired.

Nothing is illegal until you get caught.

Too many freaks, not enough circuses!

A bartender is just a pharmacist with a limited inventory.

The more I learn, the less I understand.

Have you ever had déjà vu? Have you ever had déjà vu?

BLOOPER

Patty will share her technique of making pillowcases from used underwear with the women's Bible study.

QUOTE

My play was a complete success. The audience was a failure.—*Ashleigh Brilliant*

DAY 314

In my sociology class, we were instructed to write down answers to some questions the teacher was asking.

"Next question," the instructor said. "How would you like to be seen by the opposite sex?"

I was thinking about my answer when the young woman next to me turned and asked, "How do you spell *intellectual?*"

BLOOPER

Ash Wednesday is this Thursday, February 17.

QUOTE

If you see the world in black and white, you're missing important gray matter.—*Jack Fisher*

DAY 315

Teddy came thundering down the stairs, much to his father's annoyance. "Teddy," he called, "how many more times do I have to tell you to come downstairs quietly? Now, go back upstairs and come down like a civilized human being."

There was a silence, then Teddy reappeared in the front room.

"That's better," his father said. "Now in the future you will always come down the stairs like that."

"Okay," Teddy said. "I slid down the railing."

BLOOPER

Elder Wilson said cash is the key to ending financial woes.

QUOTE

Just because a man lacks the use of his eyes does not mean he lacks vision. —*Stevie Wonder*

DAY 316

More tot truisms:

A kindergarten teacher asked, "What is the shape of the earth?" One little girl spoke up: "According to my daddy—terrible!"

Trying to come to the aid of his father, who had been stopped by an officer for speeding, the little tyke said, "Yeah? Well, if we were speeding, so were you!"

Two kids were trying to figure out what game to play. One said, "Let's play doctor." The other said, "Good idea. You operate, and I'll sue."

I guess you can get too health conscious . . . The wife and I don't have a lot of junk food in the house. Upon eating some munchies, my grandson asked what vitamins they had in them. I told him I doubted there were any at all. He replied, wide-eyed, "You mean these are just for fun?"

BLOOPER

The parsonage, located in the town's hysterical district, may be offered for sale with a lease-back option.

QUOTE

Not everything that is more difficult is more meritorious.—*Saint Thomas Aquinas*

One weekend my friend Sally, a nurse, was looking after her six-year-old nephew when he fell off a playground slide and hit his head.

Worried that he might have a concussion, Sally checked him all night. Every hour, she'd gently shake him and ask, "What's your name?" (That's standard procedure to make sure a patient does not have a concussion.) Soon he began moaning in protest each time she entered the room.

When Sally went in at 5:00 a.m., she found something white on her nephew's forehead. Leaning close, she saw a crayon-scrawled message that read, "My name is Daniel."

BLOOPER

Lt. Davis from the city police department will speak to the youth group and discuss his duties such as computer usage and finger painting.

QUOTE

No one knows what they would do in a moment of crisis, and hypothetical questions get hypothetical answers.—*Joan Baez*

DAY 318

Punny books:

The Human Brain by Sara Bellum
Please Don't Hurt Me by I. Bruce Easily
The Proper Use of Sunscreens by Justin Casey Burns
How to Cure Scratching by Ivan Awfulich
Discount Alternatives by Robin Stuff
How to Save Time by Terry A. While
How to Write Small Books by Warren Peace
The Art of Archery by Beau N. Arrow
Irish Heart Surgery by Angie O'Plasty
Desert Crossing by I. Rhoda Camel
School Truancy by Marcus Absent
The Cloakroom Attendant by Mahatma Coate
I Lost My Balance by Eileen Dover and Phil Down
Positive Reinforcement by Wade Ago
Shhh! by Danielle Soloud
Things to Do at a Party by Bob Frapples
Stop Arguing by Xavier Breath
Raising Mosquitos by I. Itch
Mountain Climbing by Hugo First

BLOOPER

The seniors' menu will be chicken cache tory and vegetables.

QUOTE

What is true by lamplight is not always true by sunlight.—*Joseph Joubert*

DAY 319

I was out walking with my four-year-old daughter. She picked up something off the ground and started to put it in her mouth. I took the item away and asked her not to do that.

"Why?" my daughter asked.

"Because it's been lying outside, you don't know where it's been, and it's dirty and probably has germs," I replied.

My daughter looked at me with total admiration and said, "Wow! How do you know all this stuff?"

I thought quickly. "Uh . . . all moms know this stuff. It's on the mommy test. You have to know it or they don't let you be a mommy." We walked along in silence for two or three minutes, but she was evidently pondering this new information.

"Oh, I get it!" she said. "So if you don't pass the test, you have to be the daddy."

BLOOPER	QUOTE
The Sunday school class went to Aunt Linda's Fudge House, where they tried to guess the height and weight of the 3-foot, 20-pound chocolate bunny.	I can't say as ever I was lost, but I was bewildered once for three days. —*Daniel Boone*

It was a difficult subject to bring before his aged mother, but Bert felt that he must. "Mom, you're no longer a spring chicken, and you do need to think of what'll happen in the future. Why don't we make arrangements about when . . . you know . . . when you pass on?"

His mother didn't say anything, just sat there staring ahead.

"I mean . . . Mom, how do you want to finally go? Do you want to be buried? Cremated?"

There was another long pause. Then his mother looked up and said, "Son, why don't you surprise me?"

BLOOPER	QUOTE
Mrs. Rice spoke about her twenty years as a Bible class eduencator.	The devil can cite Scripture for his purpose.—*William Shakespeare*

321 More deciphering the doctor:

What the doctor says: "If it doesn't clear up in a week, give me a call."

What the doctor is thinking: *I don't know what it is. Maybe it will go away by itself.*

"That's quite a nasty-looking wound."
I think I'm going to throw up.

"This may hurt a little."
Last week two patients bit off their tongues.

"Well, we're not feeling so well today, are we?"
I'm stalling for time. Who are you and why are you here?

"This should fix you up."
The drug company slipped me some big bucks to prescribe this stuff.

"Everything seems to be normal."
Rats! I guess I can't buy that new beach condo after all.

"I'd like to run some more tests."
I can't figure out what's wrong. Maybe the kid in the lab can solve this one.

"There is a lot of that going around."
That's the third one this week! I'd better learn something about this.

"If those symptoms persist, call for an appointment."
I've never heard of anything so disgusting. Thankfully I'm off next week.

BLOOPER

Free prostate cancer screening on the front steps of the church.

QUOTE

Saint: a dead sinner revised and edited.

322 The students at a school were asked to write about the harmful effects of oil on fish.

One eleven-year-old wrote, "When my mom opened a tin of sardines last night, it was full of oil and all the sardines were dead."

Correction: The recipe for the one-egg cake in the church cookbook was written as needing two eggs. It actually needs three.

Thunder is good, thunder is impressive; but it is lightning that does the work.—*Mark Twain*

·DAY·
323

Analogies and metaphors found from eleventh-grade essays:

John and Mary had never met. They were like two hummingbirds who had also never met.

Even in his last years, Grandpappy had a mind like a steel trap, only one that had been left out so long it had rusted shut.

Shots rang out, as shots are wont to do.

The plan was simple, like my brother-in-law Phil. But unlike Phil, this plan just might work.

The young fighter had a hungry look, the kind you get from not eating for a while.

He was as lame as a duck. Not the metaphorical lame duck either, but a real duck that was actually lame. Maybe from stepping on a land mine or something.

It was an American tradition, like fathers chasing kids with power tools.

He was deeply in love. When she spoke, he thought he heard bells, as if she were a garbage truck backing up.

Her eyes were like limpid pools, only they had forgotten to put in any pH cleanser.

She walked into my office like a centipede with ninety-eight missing legs.

Church bulletin board—For sale: Brand-new "Hooked on Phoenix" system for the kids.

What was most significant about the lunar landing was not that men set foot on the moon but that they set eye on the earth.—*Norman Cousins*

· DAY ·
324

In our examination paper, the professor wanted us to sign a form stating that we had not received any outside assistance. Unsure of whether he should sign the form, a student stated that he had prayed for the assistance of God.

The professor carefully studied the answer script and then said, "You can sign it with a clear conscience. God did not assist you."

BLOOPER

The annual meat pie supper will be held Friday to support the animals and Pet Partners.

QUOTE

The tyrant dies and his rule ends. The martyr dies and his rule begins.
—*Søren Kierkegaard*

· DAY ·
325

My teenager was headed to school one morning when I told him that the neck tag on his shirt was hanging out.

"I know," he replied. "It's a fad me and some of the guys started."

Weeks later, as the style persisted, I commented, "I can't stand it! Every time I see that, I want to fix it for you." I gently tucked the tag in place and rumpled his hair.

"Yeah," he said, smiling slyly. "All the girls do too."

BLOOPER

Dick Rivers said his company is looking for a quality assurance manager.

QUOTE

I never ask God to give me anything; I only ask him to put me where things are.—*Mexican proverb*

· DAY · 326

A mother takes her son to a psychiatrist and says, "Doctor, I'd like you to evaluate my thirteen-year-old son."

The doctor says, "He's suffering from transient psychosis with an intermittent rage disorder, punctuated by episodic radical mood swings, but his prognosis is good for full recovery."

"How can you say all that without even meeting him?" the mom asks.

"Didn't you say he was thirteen?"

BLOOPER

Enjoy our Italian Delight Night! All recipes are made from real Italian people.

QUOTE

If you cry "Forward," you must make plain in what direction to go. —*Anton Chekhov*

· DAY · 327

Gordon had been a faithful Christian and was in the hospital, near death. The family called their preacher to stand with them.

As the preacher stood next to the bed, Gordon's condition appeared to deteriorate, and he motioned frantically for something to write on. The preacher handed him a pen and a piece of paper, and Gordon used his last bit of energy to scribble a note, then stiffened and died. The preacher thought it best not to look at the note at that time, so he placed it in his jacket pocket.

At the funeral, as he was finishing the message, he realized that he was wearing the same jacket he'd been wearing when Gordon died. He said, "You know, our dear friend Gordon handed me a note just before he died. I haven't looked at it, but knowing Gordon, I'm sure there's a word of inspiration there for us all."

He opened the note and read, "Please move, you big lummox—you're standing on my oxygen tube!"

BLOOPER

The Women's Auxiliary Luncheon will feature bacon, lettuce, and tomato sandwiches made with bacon, lettuce, and tomato.

QUOTE

A full heart has room for everything, and an empty heart has room for nothing. —*Antonio Porchia*

· DAY · 328

There was a lawyer on vacation whose sailboat capsized in dangerous, shark-infested waters. He surprised his traveling companions by volunteering to swim to the far-off shore for help. As he swam, his companions saw two dorsal fins—great white sharks—heading straight toward him.

To their surprise, the sharks allowed the lawyer to take hold of their fins, and they escorted him safely to shore.

When the lawyer returned with help, his companions asked him how he had managed such an incredible feat. The lawyer answered, "Professional courtesy."

BLOOPER

The church will be installing new in-sulted glass windows.

QUOTE

The best rose bush, after all, is not that which has the fewest thorns, but that which bears the finest roses.—*Henry Van Dyke*

· DAY · 329

Golf truisms:

An interesting thing about golf is that no matter how badly you play, it is always possible to get worse.

Golf's a hard game to figure. One day you'll go out and slice it and shank it, hit into all the traps, and miss every green. The next day you'll go out and for no reason at all you'll really stink.

If your best shots are the practice swing and the "gimme" putt, you might wish to reconsider this game.

Golf is the only sport where the most feared opponent is you.

Golf is like marriage. If you take yourself too seriously, it won't work, and it's expensive.

The best wood in most amateurs' bags is the pencil.

BLOOPER

Homeschool student suspended.

QUOTE

All men have a reason, but not all men can give a reason.—*John Henry Cardinal Newman*

The graveside service had just barely finished when there was a massive clap of thunder followed by a tremendous bolt of lightning, accompanied by even more thunder rumbling in the distance.

The little old man looked at the pastor and calmly said, "Well, she's there."

BLOOPER

Hispanics ace Spanish tests—push up the AP scores countywide.

QUOTE

Plagiarists, at least, have the merit of preservation.—*Benjamin Disraeli*

The telephone solicitor selling basement waterproofing must have thought she'd died and gone to heaven when she reached my very polite and patient son on the phone. At the end of her long sales pitch, she asked, "Do you mind if we send out someone to give you an estimate?"

"Not at all," my son said.

"When would be a good time?" she asked.

My son answered, "Just as soon as I dig a basement."

BLOOPER

Dean Teegers explained to the Sunday school class that his attorney group gave the poor legal advice.

QUOTE

The answer to poverty is not charity, the solution to abortion is not laws, the key to saving the environment is not recycling. As Thoreau so wisely noted, we must strike at the root, not hack at the branches.—*Tere Saudavel*

·DAY·

332

On a business trip to India, Robert arrived at the airport in Delhi and took a taxi to his hotel, where he was greeted by his knowledgeable and hospitable Indian host.

The cab driver requested the equivalent of eight US dollars for the fare. It seemed reasonable, so Robert started to hand him the money. But his host exploded, grabbed the bills, and initiated a verbal assault on the cabby, calling him a worthless parasite and a disgrace to their country for trying to overcharge visitors. Robert's host threw half the amount at the driver and told him never to return. As the taxi sped off, the host gave Robert the remaining bills and asked, "How was your trip?"

"Fine," Robert replied. "Until you chased the cab away with my luggage in the trunk."

BLOOPER

Justice Marshall, a member of St. John's, will preside over the case. He said the juvenile court will try shooting defendant this time.

QUOTE

A child on a farm sees a plane fly overhead and dreams of a faraway place. A traveler on the plane sees the farmhouse below and dreams of home.

·DAY·

333

One day, Adam sat outside the Garden of Eden shortly after eating the fruit and wondered about men and women. Looking up to the heavens, he said, "Excuse me, God, can I ask you a few questions?"

God replied, "Go on, Adam, but be quick. I have a world to look after."

"When you created Eve, why did you make her body so curved and tender, unlike mine?" Adam asked.

"I did that, Adam, so you could love her."

"Oh, well then, why did you give her long, shiny, beautiful hair, and not me?"

"I did that, Adam, so you could love her."

"Oh, well then, why did you make her so stupid? Certainly not so that I could love her?"

"Well, Adam, no. I did that so she could love you."

BLOOPER

Pleasant Valley Baptist has set up a fund for beating victim's kin.

QUOTE

Complete possession is proved only by giving. All you are unable to give possesses you.—*Andre Gide*

DAY 334

At the Henry Street Hebrew School, the rabbi finished the day's lesson. It was now time for the usual question period.

"Rabbi," little Melvin asked, "there's something I need to know."

"What's that, my child?" the rabbi asked.

"Well, according to the Scriptures, the children of Israel crossed the Red Sea, right?"

"Right."

"And the children of Israel beat up the Philistines, right?"

"Uh—right."

"And the children of Israel built the temple, right?"

"Again you are correct."

"And the children of Israel fought the Egyptians, and the children of Israel were always doing something important, right?"

"All that is correct," the rabbi said. "So what's your question?"

"What I need to know is this," Melvin said. "What were all the grown-ups doing?"

BLOOPER

Our association of church schools has joined others with the goal of wiping out literacy.

QUOTE

A blade of grass is no easier to make than an oak.—*James Russell Lowell*

DAY 335

Some farmers were standing around shooting the breeze one day when the topic came around to animals and their distinguishing traits. The group agreed that the dog was probably the most loyal animal and the mule was undoubtedly the most stubborn.

Farmer Jones piped in, "You know, I believe probably the friendliest animal in all God's creation is the goose."

The others wanted to know how he'd arrived at such a conclusion.

"Well," Farmer Jones said, "I was out standing in my corn the other day, and a whole flock of 'em came by overhead. And do you know, every single one honked and waved!"

BLOOPER

Be careful out there over the Labor Day weekend. Autos are killing over 110 people a day. Let's all resolve to do better.

QUOTE

If a man could have half his wishes, he would double his trouble.—*Benjamin Franklin*

DAY 336

A little girl asked her father, "Daddy, do all fairy tales begin with 'Once upon a time'?"

He replied, "No, a whole series of fairy tales begins with 'If elected, I promise . . .'"

BLOOPER

The Christian youth group of Allegheny County will host a sundae night, featuring homemade ice cream and golden, ripe, boneless bananas.

QUOTE

For many men, the acquisition of wealth does not end their troubles, it only changes them.—*Seneca*

DAY 337

After being with his blind date all evening, the man couldn't take another minute. Earlier, he had secretly arranged to have a friend call him on the restaurant phone so he would have an excuse to leave if something like this happened.

When he returned to the table, he lowered his eyes, put on a grim expression, and said, "I have some bad news. My grandfather just died and I have to leave."

"Thank heaven!" his date replied. "If yours hadn't, mine would have had to."

BLOOPER

"There have been injuries and deaths on the mission field due to accidents last year," insurance expert Bert Foreman said, "but none of them were serious."

QUOTE

It is easier to ask forgiveness than it is to ask permission.

·DAY·
338

This guy was so lonely that he decided life would be more fun if he had a pet. So he went to the pet store and told the owner that he wanted to buy an unusual pet. After some discussion, he finally bought a centipede, which came in a little white box to use for its house.

He took the box home, found a good location for the box, and decided he would start off by taking his new pet to the coffee shop for a drink. He asked the centipede in the box, "Would you like to go grab some coffee with me?"

But there was no answer from his new pet. This bothered him a bit, but he waited a few minutes and then asked again, "How about going to the coffee shop and having a latte with me?"

Again there was no answer from his new friend and pet. So he waited a few minutes more, thinking about the situation. He decided to ask one more time, this time putting his face up against the centipede's house and shouting, "Hey in there! Would you like to go to the coffee shop and have a latte with me?"

A little voice came out of the box: "I heard you the first time! I'm putting my shoes on!"

BLOOPER

Parents who bring their strollers can store them in the alcove off the narthex. Be sure to remove your baby first.

QUOTE

The real voyage of discovery consists not in seeking new landscapes, but in having new eyes.—*Marcel Proust*

·DAY· 339

The village blacksmith finally found an apprentice willing to work hard for long hours. The blacksmith immediately began his instructions to the lad: "When I take the shoe out of the fire, I'll lay it on the anvil, and when I nod my head, you hit it with this hammer."

The apprentice did just as he was told. Now he's the village blacksmith.

BLOOPER

Pastor Geldorf paced the platform with his hands in his pockets while gesturing dramatically to the audience.

QUOTE

What we see depends mainly on what we look for.—*John Lubbock*

·DAY· 340

A group of forty-year-old girlfriends discussed where they should meet for lunch. Finally, it was agreed that they should meet at the Ocean View restaurant because the waiters there were very good-looking.

Ten years later, at fifty years of age, the group again discussed where they should meet for lunch. Finally, it was agreed that they should meet at the Ocean View restaurant because the food there was very good and the waiters were cute.

Ten years later, at sixty years of age, the group once again discussed where they should meet for lunch. Finally, it was agreed that they should meet at the Ocean View restaurant because they could eat there in peace and quiet, the restaurant had a beautiful view of the ocean, and the waiters were sweet boys.

Ten years later, at seventy years of age, the group once again discussed where they should meet for lunch. Finally, it was agreed that they should meet at the Ocean View restaurant because the restaurant was wheelchair accessible, it had an elevator, and the waiters were kindly.

Ten years later, at eighty years of age, the group once again discussed where they should meet for lunch. Finally, it was agreed that they should meet at the Ocean View restaurant because they had never been there before.

"I want the entire congregation to concentrate on one word the rest of this year, and one word only," Pastor Weeks said. "And that word is *living holy*."

When a dog runs at you, whistle for him.—*Henry David Thoreau*

· DAY ·
341

A lion woke up one morning feeling rowdy and mean. He went out, cornered a small monkey, and roared, "Who is mightiest of all jungle animals?"

The trembling monkey answered, "You are, mighty lion!"

Later, the lion confronted an ox and fiercely bellowed, "Who is the mightiest of all jungle animals?"

The terrified ox stammered, "Oh, great lion, you are the mightiest animal in the jungle!"

On a roll now, the lion swaggered up to an elephant and roared, "Who is mightiest of all jungle animals?"

Fast as lightning, the elephant snatched up the lion with his trunk and slammed him against a tree half a dozen times, leaving the lion feeling as if he'd been run over by a safari wagon. The elephant then stomped on the lion until he looked like a corn tortilla and ambled away.

The lion let out a moan of pain, lifted his head weakly, and hollered after the elephant, "Just because you don't know the answer, you don't have to get so upset about it!"

Bill Gilroy and Patsy Dellon—a twenty-year friendship ends at the altar.

Destiny has two ways of crushing us—by refusing our wishes and by fulfilling them.—*Henri Frederic Amiel*

· DAY ·
342

"Sir, I understand you admit to having broken into the dress shop four times," the judge said.

"Yes, Your Honor," the suspect replied.

"What did you steal?" the judge asked.

"I stole a dress, Your Honor."

"One dress?" the judge bellowed. "But you've admitted to breaking in four times!"

"Yes, Your Honor," the suspect said with a sigh, "but the first three times my wife didn't like the color!"

BLOOPER

Peabody Methodist Church will be presenting their ever-popular barnyard manager scene—and there will be animals on display nearby.

QUOTE

The reverse side also has a reverse side.—*Japanese proverb*

· DAY ·
343

An aged farmer and his wife were leaning against the edge of their pigpen when the old woman wistfully recalled that the next week would mark their golden wedding anniversary.

"Let's have a party, Homer," she suggested. "Let's kill a pig."

The farmer scratched his grizzled head. "Gee, Ethel," he finally said, "I don't see why the pig should take the blame for something that happened fifty years ago."

BLOOPER

In a talk to the Keenagers, Dr. Wills said that "do not resuscitate" orders often put patients at greater risk of death.

QUOTE

Each moment is a place you've never been.—*Mark Strand*

Grandpa was celebrating his one hundredth birthday, and everyone complimented him on how athletic and well-preserved he appeared. "Gentlemen, I will tell you the secret of my success," he said. "I have been in the open air day after day for some seventy-five years now."

The celebrants were impressed and asked how he managed to keep up his rigorous fitness regimen. "Well, you see, my wife and I were married seventy-five years ago. On our wedding night, we made a solemn pledge. Whenever we had a fight, the one who was proved wrong would go outside and take a walk."

BLOOPER

Church bulletin board—For sale: A two-carat embezzled diamond ring. Beautiful.

QUOTE

Finish last in the race and they call you a loser. Finish last in medical school and they call you a doctor.—*Abe Lemons*

Four men—a mechanical engineer, an electrical engineer, a chemical engineer, and a computer engineer—were riding in a car when it stalled.

The mechanical engineer said, "It must be the pistons; let's repair them and be on our way."

The electrical engineer said, "It has to be the spark plugs; we'll replace them and be ready to roll in no time at all."

The chemical engineer said, "No, it has to be bad gas; we'll flush the system and be on our way."

The three of them turned to the computer engineer. "What do you think we should do?" they asked.

The computer engineer shrugged and said, "Let's get out of the car, close the doors, get back in, and try restarting it."

BLOOPER

The deaf ministry of Gospel Outreach will hold a silent auction this Saturday.

QUOTE

A hole is nothing at all, but you can still break your neck in it.

· DAY ·

346

A Scout master was teaching his Boy Scouts about survival in the desert. "What are the three most important things you should bring with you in case you get lost in the desert?" he asked. Several hands went up, and many important things were suggested, such as food and matches.

Then one little boy in the back eagerly raised his hand. "Yes, Davey, what are the three most important things you would bring with you?" the Scout master asked.

Davey replied, "A compass, a canteen of water, and a deck of cards."

"Why is that, Davey?" the Scout master asked.

"Well," Davey said, "the compass is to find the right direction, and the water is to prevent dehydration."

"And what about the deck of cards?" the Scout master asked impatiently.

Davey replied, "Well, sir, as soon as you start playing solitaire, someone is bound to come up behind you and say, 'Put that red nine on top of that black ten.'"

BLOOPER

Church bulletin board: Three out of five marriages end in divorce. Don't spend a fortune on your reception. Celebrate at the Fountains Reception Center and save.

QUOTE

Perhaps there should be one day a week when you tackle your "Things I Have to Undo" list.

· DAY ·

347

As US tourists in Israel, Morris and his wife, Ruth, were sitting outside a Bethlehem souvenir shop, waiting for fellow tourists. An Arab salesman approached them carrying belts. After an impassioned sales talk yielded no results, he asked where they were from.

"America," Morris replied.

Looking at Ruth's dark hair and olive skin, the Arab responded, "She's not from the States."

"Yes, I am," Ruth said.

He asked her, "Is he your husband?"

"Yes," she replied.

Turning to Morris, the Arab said, "She is very beautiful. I'll give you one hundred camels for her."

Morris looked stunned, and there was a long silence.

"I will give you two hundred camels for the delightful creature."

Finally, Morris shook his head and replied, "She's not for sale."

After the salesman left, the somewhat indignant Ruth asked, "Morris, what took you so long to answer?"

Morris replied, "I was trying to figure out how to get two hundred camels back home."

BLOOPER

Bridgeport Church will host a *Polar Express* party, complete with music, train rides, Satan, and hot chocolate. Great for your whole family.

QUOTE

Everyone is a genius. But if you judge a fish by its ability to climb a tree, it will spend its whole life believing it is stupid.—*Albert Einstein*

·DAY·
348

My friend wanted a boat more than anything. His wife kept refusing, but he bought one anyway.

"I'll tell you what," he told her. "In the spirit of compromise, why don't you name the boat?" Being a good sport, she accepted.

When her husband went to the dock for the maiden voyage, this is the name he saw painted on the side: "For Sale."

BLOOPER

Church bulletin board—For sale: Rabbis, hamsters, and guinea pigs.

QUOTE

I don't know the key to success, but I know the key to failure is trying to please everyone.—*Bill Cosby*

·DAY·

349 Have you heard about the lawyer's word processor?
No matter what font you select, everything comes out in fine print.

BLOOPER

Fire Chief Stone spoke to our seniors and said they should all remember the "Five Ps" of cold-weather safety: protecting people, protecting plants, protecting pets, protecting pxposed pipes, and practicing pire pafety.

QUOTE

There are always three sides to every story: your side, the other side, and the truth.

·DAY·

350 My father was completely lost in the kitchen and never ate unless someone prepared a meal for him. When Mother was ill, however, he volunteered to go to the supermarket for her. She sent him off with a carefully numbered list of seven items.

Dad returned shortly, very proud of himself, and proceeded to unpack the grocery bags. He had one bag of sugar, two dozen eggs, three hams, four boxes of detergent, five boxes of crackers, six eggplants, and seven green peppers.

BLOOPER

Church bulletin board—For sale: 2003 Pontiac Grandma SE.

QUOTE

It isn't the mountains ahead that wear you out, it's the grain of sand in your shoe.

A college professor at a small liberal arts college in Ohio removed a tennis ball from his jacket pocket as he walked into the lecture hall each morning. He would set it on the corner of the podium. After giving the lecture for the day, he would pick up the tennis ball, place it in his jacket pocket, and leave the room.

No one understood why he did this, until one day when a student fell asleep during the lecture. The professor didn't miss a word of his lecture while he walked over to the podium, picked up the tennis ball, and threw it, hitting the sleeping student squarely on top of the head.

The next day, the professor walked into the room, reached into his jacket, and removed a baseball.

No one fell asleep in his class the rest of the semester.

BLOOPER

St. Peter's Academy is offering courses for the new student. Need to upgrade for collage? Try one of our night classes.

QUOTE

I don't see how an article of clothing can be indecent. A person, yes.

A man rushed to the jewelry counter in the store where I work soon after the doors opened one morning and said he needed a pair of diamond earrings. I showed him a wide selection, and quickly he picked out a pair.

When I asked him if he wanted the earrings gift wrapped, he said, "That'd be great. But can you make it quick? I forgot today was my anniversary, and my wife thinks I'm taking out the trash."

BLOOPER

We wish all our Jewish friends a happy Chankkuak.

QUOTE

Travelers never think they are the foreigners.—*Mason Cooley*

DAY 353

We telemarketers know we're universally loathed. Still, some people are quite pleasant on the phone.

One day I called a number and asked to speak with Mr. Morgan. The woman who answered explained that he no longer lived at that address, but she did have a number where he could be reached.

I thanked her, rang that number, and was greeted with, "Good morning, Highland View Cemetery."

BLOOPER

Junior Women will host a chili supper —made from the original chili dog owner Lucile.

QUOTE

A liberal is a conservative who's been arrested. A conservative is a liberal who's been mugged.—*Wendy Kaminer*

DAY 354

The drill sergeant, making his morning announcements to a group of newcomers in a training camp, stated, "Today, gentlemen, I have some good news and some bad news. First, the good. Private Johnson will be setting the pace on our morning run."

The platoon was overjoyed, as Private Johnson was overweight and terribly slow. But then the drill sergeant finished his statement: "Now for the bad news. Private Johnson will be driving a truck."

BLOOPER

While on their summer missions trip to Rome, our students stayed in a hotel less than a block from the Eiffel Tower.

QUOTE

I always thought a yard was three feet, then I started mowing the lawn.

I was meeting a friend in a restaurant, and as I went in, I noticed two pretty girls looking at me.

"Nine," I heard one whisper as I passed.

Feeling pleased with myself, I swaggered over to my buddy and told him a girl had just rated me a nine out of ten.

"I don't want to ruin it for you," he said, "but when I walked in, they were speaking German."

BLOOPER

The Ladies' Auxiliary of St. Ann's is hosting a "Help Fight a Cancer Patient" event.

QUOTE

It is not the man who has little, but he who desires more, that is poor.
—*Seneca*

At the height of a political corruption trial, the prosecuting attorney attacked a witness. "Isn't it true," he bellowed, "that you accepted five thousand dollars to compromise this case?"

The witness stared out the window as though he hadn't heard the question.

"Isn't it true that you accepted five thousand dollars to compromise this case?" the lawyer repeated.

The witness still did not respond.

Finally, the judge leaned over and said, "Sir, please answer the question."

"Oh," the startled witness said, "I thought he was talking to you."

BLOOPER

The seminar on pay equality is $5 for women and $6.50 for men. A continental breakfast is included.

QUOTE

A hen is only an egg's way of making another egg.—*Samuel Butler*

• DAY •
357

Jose rides up to the Mexican border on his bicycle. He has two large bags over his shoulders. A guard stops him and says, "What's in the bags?"

"Sand," Jose says.

"We'll just see about that," the guard says. "Get off the bike."

The guard takes the bags and empties them out but finds nothing in them but sand. He detains Jose overnight and has the sand analyzed, only to discover that there is nothing but pure sand in the bags. The guard releases Jose and lets him cross the border with the sand.

A week later, the same thing happens. The guard asks, "What have you got?"

"Sand," Jose says.

The guard does his thorough examination and discovers that the bags contain nothing but sand. He gives the sand back to Jose, and Jose crosses the border on his bicycle.

This sequence of events repeats every week for ten years. Then one day, Jose doesn't show up. The guard is overcome with curiosity and goes into Mexico to look for him. He finds him at a cantina, just over the border.

"Hey, Jose," the guard says, "I know you've been smuggling something. It's driving me crazy. It's all I think about. I'm retiring tomorrow, so it doesn't matter now. But just between you and me, what were you smuggling?"

Jose says, "Bicycles."

BLOOPER

The parish is involved in a lawsuit—they are charging that the campers at the deaf camp across the road from the church are making too much noise.

QUOTE

There is only one pretty child in the world, and every mother has it.

—*Chinese proverb*

• DAY •
358

A biker is riding a new motorcycle on the highway. He pulls next to a car and knocks on the window. The driver opens the window. "Yes?"

"Ever driven a Honda motorcycle?"

"No, I haven't."

The biker drives on until he sees another car and knocks on the window. The driver opens the window. "Yes?"

"Ever driven a Honda motorcycle?"

"No, I haven't."

Then suddenly there is a curve, and the biker sees it too late. He crashes off the road into a ditch. A car stops, and a man runs to the unlucky biker.

Bruised and battered, the biker asks, "Ever driven a Honda motorcycle?"

"Yes, I have. I had a Honda for twenty years."

The biker says, "Tell me, where are the brakes?"

BLOOPER

Church bulletin board—For sale: Three-piece couch set. Good condition. Manure color. Will deliver.

QUOTE

Every exit is an entrance somewhere else.—*Tom Stoppard*

·DAY·
359

The policeman came upon a banged-up and bloody man lying by the curb. There was glass all around him—from a broken headlight, most likely. The police did notice that there were no skid marks—meaning, perhaps, that the driver of the car had not seen the pedestrian.

The policeman knelt next to the injured man, who said, "It happened so fast. The car hit me from behind." The man coughed a bit, then added, "You have to arrest my mother-in-law."

"But you said the car hit you from behind," the officer said. "How could you tell it was your mother-in-law?"

"I recognized the laugh!"

BLOOPER

Our Luther League delegates will join young people from fifty-four states and three foreign countries when they meet this month in Dallas.

QUOTE

A pedestal is as much a prison as any small space.—*Gloria Steinem*

·DAY·
360

My fourteen-year-old son and I were lying on our backs on the grass in the park, watching the clouds loiter overhead, when he asked me, "Dad, why are we here?"

And this is what I said:

"I've thought a lot about it, son, and I don't think it's all that complicated. I think maybe we're here just to teach a kid how to bunt or how to eat sunflower seeds without using his hands.

"We're here to wear our favorite sweat-soaked Boston Red Sox cap and the Converse sneakers we lettered in on a Saturday morning, with nowhere we have to go and no one special we have to be.

"I don't think the meaning of life is worrying over what comes after death but tasting all the tiny moments that come before it. We're here to be there when our kid has three goals and an assist. And especially when he doesn't.

"See, grown-ups spend so much time slaving toward the better car, the perfect house, the big day that will finally make them happy, when happy just walked by wearing a bicycle helmet two sizes too big for him. We're not here to find a way to heaven. The way is heaven.

"Does that answer your question, son?"

"Not really, Dad," he said.

"No?"

And he said, "No, what I meant is, why are we here when Mom said to pick her up forty minutes ago?"

BLOOPER

Betsy Geotz, president of the Watertown Human Society, wants to remind all friends that the Human Society will host the annual pig roast this weekend. Tickets are still available.

QUOTE

If I asked people what they wanted, they would have said faster horses.
—*Henry Ford*

·DAY· 361

A friend and his wife were considering traveling to Alaska for a trip that the husband had long dreamed of taking. He kept talking about how great it would be to stay in a log cabin without electricity, to hunt moose, and to drive a dog team instead of a car.

"If we decided to live there permanently, away from civilization, what would you miss the most?" he asked his wife.

She replied, "You."

BLOOPER

Visiting nurse Shilds told our seniors that to reduce the risk of being bitten by mosquitoes, she recommends that people should attempt to avoid being bitten by mosquitoes.

QUOTE

There has never been a good war, or a bad peace.—*Benjamin Franklin*

·DAY· 362

A man wanted to buy a horse from a farmer whose command of the English language was limited. The man told the farmer he wanted to buy a "good-looking horse."

They walked to the stable, and the buyer pointed to a specific horse that he wanted to buy.

"But that is not a good-looking horse," the farmer said.

"But it is a good-looking horse," the buyer replied.

"No, it is not a good-looking horse!" the farmer insisted.

In spite of the farmer's protests, and thinking that beauty is in the eye of the beholder, the buyer bought the horse.

The next day he returned, furious, saying, "That horse you sold me is blind!"

The farmer replied, "I told you it is not a good-looking horse!"

BLOOPER

Church bulletin board—For sale: Genuine muslin-wrapped coil spring mattress. Never used.

QUOTE

The greatest griefs are those we cause ourselves.—*Sophocles*

· DAY ·
363

As the bus pulled away, I realized I had left my purse under the seat. Later I called the company and was relieved that the driver had found my bag. When I went to pick it up, several off-duty bus drivers surrounded me. One man handed me my purse, two typewritten pages, and a box containing the contents of my purse.

"We're required to inventory lost wallets and purses," he explained. "I think you'll find everything there."

As I started to put my belongings back into the purse, the man continued, "I hope you don't mind if we watch. Even though we all tried, none of us could fit everything into your purse. And we'd like to see just how you do it."

BLOOPER

George Glenn, the church's one-man band, has gotten back together.

QUOTE

Science is organized knowledge. Wisdom is organized life.—*Immanuel Kant*

· DAY ·
364

Being the office supervisor, Mr. Thaddock had to have a word with a new employee who never arrived at work on time. The supervisor explained that her tardiness was unacceptable and that other employees had noticed that she was walking in late every day.

After listening to Mr. Thaddock's complaints, she agreed that this was a problem and even offered a solution. "Is there another door I could use?"

BLOOPER

The Walk for Fitness group will host an all-you-can-eat pancake fund-raiser at the church in March.

QUOTE

Assumptions are the termites of relationships.

A store that sells husbands has just opened in New York City. Among the instructions at the entrance is a description of how the store operates: You may visit the store only once. There are six floors, and the attributes of the men increase as you ascend each floor. There is, however, a catch: you may choose any man from a particular floor, or you may choose to go up a floor, but you cannot go back down except to exit the building.

A woman goes to the Husband Store to find a husband. On the first floor, the sign on the door reads: "Floor 1—These men have jobs and love the Lord." The second-floor sign reads: "Floor 2—These men have jobs, love the Lord, and love kids." The third-floor sign reads: "Floor 3—These men have jobs, love the Lord, love kids, and are extremely good-looking." *Wow*, she thinks, but feels compelled to keep going. On the fourth floor, the sign reads: "Floor 4—These men have jobs, love the Lord, love kids, are drop-dead gorgeous, and help with the housework."

"Oh, mercy me!" she exclaims. "What could be better than that?" Still, she goes to the fifth floor, and the sign reads: "Floor 5—These men have jobs, love the Lord, love kids, are drop-dead gorgeous, help with the housework, and have a strong romantic streak." She is so tempted to stay—that sounds like the perfect man—but her curiosity gets the better of her, and she goes to the sixth floor. The sign reads: "Floor 6—You are visitor 4,363,012 on this floor. There are no men on this floor. This floor exists solely as proof that women are impossible to please. Thank you for shopping at the Husband Store. Watch your step as you exit the building, and have a nice day!"

BLOOPER

Mayor Spivens reminded the church people that next week will be a dumpster cleanup event. Do not place your trash at the curb. It will be violated.

QUOTE

You can't shake a hand with a clenched fist.—*Gandhi*

Jim Kraus is a 1972 graduate of the University of Pittsburgh, with a degree in English and communication arts. He attended the Paris-American Academy in France, where he learned to effectively point at various menu selections and get lost on the Metro without even trying. He also was awarded a master's degree in writing arts from DePaul University in 2008, where he learned to write much more gooder than before.

Jim has been a journalist for a small-town newspaper in southern Minnesota, has worked in sales, and was editor of a trade magazine. For the past two decades, he has been senior vice president at Tyndale House Publishers. He has a collection of some four hundred miniature souvenir buildings and loves collecting things that he can buy in tacky tourist traps. His favorite is an electrified version of the Statue of Liberty with a torch that lights up.

He and his long-suffering wife, Terri, have written ten books together, and Jim has another ten solo efforts.

The Kraus family includes Jim, Terri, their thirteen-year-old son, Elliot, and a gentle-souled miniature schnauzer, Rufus. They all coexist with an ill-tempered cat, Petey, in a suburb of Chicago.